WOODLAND
MANITOU

To Be on Earth

WOODLAND MANITOU

To Be on Earth

HEIDI BARR

Homebound Publications
Ensuring that the mainstream isn't the only stream.

Published in 2017 by Homebound Publications
Front Cover Image © Martins Vanags
Cover and Interior Designed by Leslie M. Browning
ISBN 978-1-938846-72-4
First Edition Trade Paperback

The essays "A Wild Perspective," "Jars of Bliss," and "Fading into Stillness" were first published in *Prairie Grown: Stories and Recipes from a South Dakota Hillside*. Reprinted with permission from Avenida Books.

The essay "Old Beauty" was first published in the April 2014 edition of *Minnesota Women's Press*. Reprinted with permission.

Homebound Publications
Ensuring the mainstream isn't the only stream.
WWW.HOMEBOUNDPUBLICATIONS.COM

10 9 8 7 6 5 4 3 2 1

Homebound Publications is committed to ecological stewardship. We greatly value the natural environment and invest in environmental conservation. Our books are printed on paper with chain of custody certification from the Forest Stewardship Council, Sustainable Forestry Initiative, and the Program for the Endorsement of Forest Certification.

For Eva Emmaline,
and all the other children of the earth

Contents

MANITOU

noun man·i·tou \ˈma-n ətü\
a supernatural force that according to an Algonquian
conception pervades the natural world

To Be on Earth

Through the tree cover,
prairie grasses waving
in the fading light

squeals of jubilation
over a thumb-sized toad
a bucket of soil
a crimson raspberry:

an evolving understanding
what it means to be alive
and present in this place,

seeping into the earth's breath;
through the moments
that make up a life

spent in the shade
of the brightness
in the shadow
made by the sun

and all the other things
that come
when we decide
to be on earth.

Preface

Ten years ago, I lived in the middle of an urban area. St. Paul is Minnesota's capital, and half of what Minnesotans call the Twin Cities—Minneapolis completes the picture. Boasting a population of over three million, this metro, like most cities is busy and full of people, concrete, job opportunities, wealth, poverty, loss, joy, sorrow and a myriad of other things that punctuate human existence in the modern world. Like most cities, people come from all over in search of energy to thrive on, communities in which to exist, and someplace to call home. Like most cities, it is growing. And like most cities, it can be a real challenge for the people who live there to build a life that includes getting outside and enjoying nature on a regular basis. There are opportunities in cities that don't exist in rural settings, to be sure. But there is also an ache for a way of life that follows a rhythm more ancient than the one interstate highways and artificial lights can provide. For many, life is hectic. To do lists are long. Finances are tight. Cars get the right of way. Life and creation often don't harmonize.

So which is more important? Opportunities in the city or living a life in tune with creation? For me to be living in tune with the natural world—whatever that might look like—takes priority. My life has evolved in such a way that today I live well outside the city limits, but when I did live deep in the heart of the concrete jungle, I found that harmony—that ancient rhythm of nature—by running.

I ran because it was the easiest way I could think of to get some sort of relationship going with the outdoor world while benefiting from the opportunities that came from an urban home base (without putting hundreds of miles on the car and using the fossil fuel that would have been required to drive to parks all the time). I ran around our slightly ghetto neighborhood, looking for beauty in the people that lived there, in the countless flowers that were planted along the sidewalks, and in the few trees that were allowed to stay as development went up around them. I ran around the neighborhoods surrounding my office building after dodging traffic, thankful for a chance to get out of my temperature controlled cubicle to see the light of day and feel the natural air on my skin. On the days when I worked the evening shift, I ran in the morning with a friend down at the Mississippi river bottoms, thankful for the opportunity to spend an hour amidst the swampy wildness that runs right through the middle of the metro area.

Pockets of wilderness can be few and far between in the heart of a city, but they are there. They are in the clumps of trees behind the abandoned house down the block and in the green space between the office parking lots, struggling to maintain themselves as our culture closes in on them. They are in the breeze that blows despite the pollution that likes to hitch a ride. They are in the woman behind the bank teller window and in the kid wiping down the tables at the diner despite the illusions that mar the view of who they truly are behind the cloak of employment. I ran to remind myself that being outside is what is real and what connects us to our authentic selves—it is what matters and is what holds the key to contentment, joy and fulfillment for all people, whether we are willing to recognize that or not. Years after moving outside the city, I am able to look back on my time spent living in the midst of that churning, man-made energy and be forever grateful that I took the time to get outside regularly—to acknowledge that despite the walls we put up, humans are not separate from nature. We can see it anywhere if we take the time to look. Sufi teacher Llewellyn Vaughan Lee writes, "Until we get to the root of our image of separateness, there can be no healing."

Perhaps to notice and celebrate nature, wherever we spot it, is to invite some of the healing that is so needed in the world.

These days, I can step out the front door in the morning and hear nothing but birds and wind rustling through the trees. But in the years leading up to finding the means and the opportunity to change my life situation, running outside and being intentional about noticing the wildness that can't be contained by humanity kept me sane those years I spent living in the city.

Introduction

ON THE PRAIRIE YOU ALWAYS HEAR THE FIRST THUNDER before a storm faintly, like a muffled explosion. The sky, blue just an hour ago, turns slate gray, and the sun gives in to the cloudy shadows. The ever present wind lies in wait, seeking respite before being called into service again. Thunderheads, like giant anvils, crowd together at the edge of the horizon, and lightning flashes in the distance, but the air around you is almost peaceful if you close your eyes. You know the winds will be roaring soon enough, and hail might pierce the tender leaves of the beans and cabbage leaving everyone with a garden cursing the weather in the morning. But in the moments before the storm you can lean into the stillness of this place; this landscape that soothes and torments in the same breath, this carpet of rolling tall grass that rivals the sky in its enormity. Once, in another lifetime, there was an ocean here, and if you plant your feet in the soil you can almost feel the ancients rising and falling like the tides of old as the storm gathers strength.

I've heard the prairie called "flyover country" more times than I can count, and on the hard days, anyone who lives there will agree with the claim. When life shakes because there's nothing between you and the sky to create a buffer, it's easy to assume you'll just be swept away like a tumbleweed with no control over its path. But when the day breaks cool and clear, and the winds are gentle instead of angry, you remember that this place, though it seems unforgiving, is ripe with opportunities to gather strength like a farmer gathers bushel baskets of potatoes in the fall. And on the days when you forget—everyone has those days—and the wind and the rain and the snow and the floods are screaming at you to give in and leave, or the ground lays in want of moisture, parched, cracked and brown—on those days you can look up at the sky and drink in the empty space that lets you breathe. And then the earth breathes with you as life keeps rolling across the plain.

Poet Mary Oliver writes, "The world offers itself to your imagination." No one's place in the world is set in stone. There are challenges, yes. Despair is real and familiar to all no matter what sort of landscape gets called 'home'. But the winter still comes each year, as does the spring, summer and fall. Every dew wet apple blossom, every garden plot filled with creeping flowers and weeds, each crimson leaf, each sparkle in a newly white morning—each nuance of creation offers up a sense of place and rhythm. Every creature and every piece of creation has a place in that mystery.

I grew up on the prairie, in a house my father built from rough wood and timber beams on the side of a hill overlooking the winding Big Sioux River. My three brothers and I spent our childhood roaming the fields around the house as the trees our parents planted reached further skyward with each passing year. We learned the difference between Big Bluestem and Sideoats Grama, how to plant a garden, catch a feral cat and start a fire in a wood stove. We built forts of sticks in the shelterbelt, went on grand adventures amidst the seas of prairie grass, pasque flowers and cow pies and developed a respect and reverence for the natural world. We spent countless hours enchanted by streams of spring melt, in palaces made of logs, bark and snow and rode the flooded banks of the Big Sioux River on inner tubes with wild abandon (much to our mother's dismay).

Now I live in Minnesota, a state that, like the South Dakota prairie of my youth, has four distinct seasons. As I strive to live in a way that honors sustainable ways of being for people, communities and the planet, the rhythms of the natural world have (and continue to) profoundly inform how I walk on the earth and how I perceive what I find here. I have found the seasons to provide structure in times of transition, reason to savor in times of infinite beauty and reason to hope and find joy in the present in an era that still includes great suffering. The seasons have taught me that our place on earth is at once vast and tiny. The turning of the year paints a picture showing that the world is not divided into ours and theirs, natural and man-made, or his and hers. We as creatures—members of a planetary family—are not separate from one another. There is a sense of oneness that flows through all things when we take time to notice it: a breath of awe that weaves the fabric of creation together.

This book is a compilation of essays written over a period of seven years as I settled into country living after a time spent in an urban environment. It is a collection of ideas, reflections and accounts of experiences of what has been, what is yet to come, and what is alive in the present moments. It is a glimpse into what it's like to be human on a planet that continues to support life despite our species' insistence on trying to run the show. It's a glimpse into what it's like to live in hopeful expectation, in worry that nothing will ever change (or that too much will, for the worse), and in wonder of what already has. It is a glimpse of the world through the privileged lens of a white woman in middle class America. It is but one interpretation of what it means to be on earth.

PART ONE

Spring

The deep roots never doubt spring will come.
–MARTY RUBIN

What comes to mind when you hear the word spring? In my part of the world, spring means getting out the mud boots, ordering seeds because I forgot to order them in January when you are "supposed to" and hoping for warmer weather while still mourning the passing of winter. Spring means anticipation and newness and lengthening. It means the return of bird and frog song to the morning, and it means sloughing off winter dryness and letting the sun melt into my skin. It means the first steps on freshly turned soil and life springing forth from that which seemed dead just weeks ago. It is the tiny blue wildflowers that are first to pop up and the delicate tendrils of new growth on the mossy parts of the yard. It is recognizing that the earth knows how to do this, if we would only follow her lead.

Memories

IN MY MEMORY, I walk out back behind the house to a stream. It's flowing through tall grass and around the snow that still lingers after a long winter. Water rushes by icy patches and under them, intent on its course down the gently sloping ground.

Last night the baby decided not to sleep. Sometimes she does that—wakes up every hour and then stops waking up because she also stops going back to sleep. Those nights are hard. People say we won't remember this in a few years. I wonder if that's a good thing, or not.

In my memory, I look out over the front yard and see young trees, and grass is king. The river is high, and the view from the porch is wide open and windy. There are Holsteins in the pasture across the road, and pasque flowers emerging from a long sleepy winter.

As of one month ago, there is a new house overlooking our garden. It was built by a nice retired couple who invite us in every time we stop by to say hello. I can imagine their excitement on seeing their new home come to completion as they picture living out their days on the edge of the woods and lake. I miss the open space that used to be there while we welcome them to the neighborhood.

In my memory, big and little bluestem sway in the hay field down the hill, and a row of round bales sits quietly under the last remnants of a white winter blanket. The last of the sledding tracks have melted back into the earth and the old, broken tree that stands alone gives life one more try.

This morning our little lake is a shimmering canvas of reflection as the sun rises to greet the day. Last year's leaves, curled up and tired after a season of life, are awash with the new spring light. I put the coffee on and feed the cats as the light blazes in through the kitchen window. The chocolate chips that live in a ceramic container on the counter start to melt, giving in to the heat.

In my memory, and in present time, I can walk out back, behind the house to a stream. The stream flows through tall grass, over roots and rocks, and past icy patches—always intent on its course. The trees in my memory have grown up, and the trees of the present have always been here. Pasque flowers keep emerging after their long winter slumber, and the big bluestem that is left keeps swaying, insistent on living, no matter who stakes claim on its home. The sun keeps rising, and the baby will grow up.

I want to remember.

Return of the Light

To some these days are known as Imbolc—the mid-
point between the solstice & the equinox. Always
makes me think of mid-points in journeys—time to
reassess our resources & replenish what is needed.
−ORIAH MOUNTAIN DREAMER

Today—the mid-point between winter solstice and the spring
equinox—feels like the space before the beginning. Maybe like
the ten minutes before a race starts, while milling around still in
warm-up sweats, waiting to toe the line. Maybe like the hours
spent in transit when moving away to college for the first time.
Maybe like the eight to ten days after planting tomato seeds,
before the seeds send up sprouts into the air. A bit nervous, but
excited to start running. Unsure about what the next four years
will be like, but ready for whatever comes next. Patiently letting
nature take its course and having faith that life will emerge.

We don't know exactly what this time of celebrating the return of the light will bring with it into our space. We can only
breathe, one breath at a time, one moment at a time, in the
space that we have. We can only look to our own being, to our
own essence, to find the right race to run. We remember that
we run purely to feel the wind on our skin, to know the joy in
the faces of those we run beside and to project our life energy,
our light, into the space we have. We remember that we are

worthy to run beside anyone, just as everyone else is worthy to run beside us. We remember that ours is a race with no winners and no finish line, just individual beacons of light forming a web that stretches across the planet.

In the space before the beginning, as the light returns to this part of the Earth, there is only a knowing that to begin is to continue to be in our own space and to let others be in theirs. It is to know that our space is a part of everyone else's and that we depend on them, and they on us. It is to know that we are equal and that when we honor that knowing, miracles become reality, and reality becomes anything that we can imagine.

We are in the space before the beginning, and it is okay to be here. But we don't want to be here forever—in fact, we cannot. The light returns whether we are ready for it or not.

So in this space, in this return of the light, we remember that more life waits for us when we cross the starting line. That limitless opportunities and new ways of remaining true to ourselves unfold when we pull up to our new campus. That immeasurable vibrancy and robust growth emerge when a single seed germinates and propels its being into pure life force. We know this space, the space before the beginning and the return of the light, because we have been here already. We are a part of the Earth's cycles, and we are ready. We are ready to honor the balance of what is, we lean into our own loveliness, and we welcome the wilds of our imagination to move us into a reality that invites us to bloom.

A Beautiful Mess

Spring is a messy time when you live in a state that boasts winter low temperatures of negative 30 and summer highs of 101. Contrast like that means that snow falls before winter officially arrives and stays well past the spring equinox. Contrast like that means it can be five degrees at 4am and 43 degrees six hours later as the sun regains power at the end of March. Contrast like that means melting snow turns into torrents of water screaming in joy to be moving to lower ground over still frozen ground in early April. And as May approaches, it means mud reigns on the unpaved roadways as the frost creeps up from deep in the earth, awake again after nine months of hibernation. Contrast like that means spring is eagerly awaited and dreaded in the same thought.

But along with puddles and deep rutted roads and inconvenience, it means the return of the blue heron, the robin and the loon. It means frog songs punctuating the space that was left when those voices went to sleep in the fall. It means a lake studded with diamonds as the ice acquiesces to the warmth of a spring wind. It means delicate green buds on a crab apple tree and herbs that will wait no longer to push through the soil to breathe their fragrance into the spring air. It means life renewing into a fresh version abundance that can only be felt after time without it.

And it means letting the messy and the unsettled; the light and the dark; the ease and the challenge—it means letting these things exist in a way that honors the beauty that can only be found in the transitions, in the unknown, and in the spaces that refuse to be defined by understanding.

Spring is a messy time when you live in a place where contrast has the last word. And it's a time of life, beauty, movement and waiting, all existing on the same plane as the world decides what is going to happen next.

Newness

I didn't think I wanted to write about our daughter's birth. It seems almost like a cliché topic these days with all the blogging people do, all the pregnancy/baby websites, all the stories that find their way into my life as others feel the need to share their own. But today, as the spring equinox approaches, a time when light and dark are balanced and when the earth is waking up, it feels like the right time to tell the story of one new life coming into being.

In the months leading up to my due date, I spent a lot of time learning how to "process fear." The basic gist of the short meditative practice that I did is that I would find fear in my physical body, acknowledge it, let it grow, and then imagine it being infused it with light and love. I would thank it for being part of my story and for the work it had done in my life so far, for being with me for so long. And then I would let it go, back into the source of all things. Being on good terms with fear, plus a lot of yoga and walks outside, paved the way for the birth experience that I had.

The morning that Eva decided to arrive, I woke up at 6am, ate a bowl of cereal as the sun came up over the lake and told my spouse, Nick, that we should probably go to the hospital. By 11am, the world had welcomed another squealing, rosy colored little person. Labor and delivery were certainly no picnic, and there was plenty of pain. But it was painful and hard in a way that felt manageable, productive, and worthwhile. I didn't labor at home for hours like they said we should be prepared to do. In the weeks prior to delivery day, I heard the phrase "Well, we'll put pain medication as a maybe then" when I said that pain medication wasn't part of the plan. The remarkable thing is that it was never a maybe, never even a possibility—not because we got to the hospital past the time when they can administer pain medication, (which we did) but because I believed 100% that it wasn't necessary, and I think Eva and Nick did also. There are certainly instances when medication or medical intervention are necessary, and everyone has the right to their own choices. There is no "right choice" in the birthing process—at the end of the day, everyone's goal is the same: a healthy mother and baby.

For me, the right choice was to experience everything about birth—even the painful or more difficult parts. I was able to use my practice of being intimate with fear (and the discomfort that usually comes with it) to have a natural birth. I was able to trust myself enough to be with the hard parts and breathe through them, and I was able to allow my physical body to do what it knows how to do. I am grateful that there were no complications or medical reasons for intervention.

Many well-wishers said having an epidural would make it easier to be present during labor and delivery, and that may well be true for some. It wasn't true for me. Being fully aware and being able to experience everything during Eva's birth was the only way for me to be fully present. I never got to the place where the midwife said all women get to: feeling like it isn't possible to go on and needing a full team of supporters to make it through to the end. Having support was essential, yes, and I'm thankful for the presence of Nick and the midwife. But I never thought, "I can't do this" like I was warned would happen. My body, like all women's bodies, is designed to go through the process of labor and delivery of a baby. The sensations—all of them—were simply part of it, something to acknowledge, accept and let be there. Masking the pain or being afraid of it wouldn't have been true to how Eva needed to arrive. She wanted to be born without complication, and she wanted a mother who felt empowered and capable of bringing her into the world. Truth be told, I think she helped me from wherever souls are before they fully arrive. Her birth was what she needed for her soul to fully arrive as a little human.

So during these days of anticipating the return of spring, we celebrate new life, get rid of negative energy and plan for what is to come. Eva's newness is a reminder of how we can look toward the rising sun each day and stay present and awake despite the illusions that sometimes taint the view.

Hues of Violet

The first day of spring this year felt like an ordinary day. It was yesterday. A mid-week day. Wednesdays for me are typically spent with my daughter Eva, doing things that toddlers like to do. We ate peach coffee cake for breakfast, passed a red ball back and forth countless times, crawled around on the living room furniture, paged through books, napped and did it again in the afternoon. It seemed like any other Wednesday. Any other ordinary day. The temperature never got above 25 degrees, and the wind that had been blowing from the west continued, full force. We stayed inside. The day was bright, and it was hard to look out at the brilliant lingering whiteness without squinting and looking away. As Eva and I moved through our afternoon and then evening routine, so too did the sun as it moved across the sky and set for the first time in a new season. A line of orange-yellow haze started to outline the horizon, and then out from under a line of rogue clouds came a brightness as the sun found an opening to shine through in full once more. As it sank down behind the hills, hues of violet filled the skyline, and it was like the earth had opened herself fully to be saturated with light.

The equinox provides a space for growth and transition— light and dark balance, and we look forward to longer days and warming temperatures. Today, on the second day of spring, the earth has started to move out of hibernation, and has fully exhaled the breath she'd been holding. Today is still. The wind of the past three days has ceased, and the air holds a sense of quiet, calm energy. Perhaps the earth knows that we are now ready to use the breath she held for us all winter.

Yesterday felt like an ordinary day in many ways, and rightly so. Through the ordinary comes waves of abundance, joy and peace, as we inhale what the earth and all of Creation has to offer and exhale our interpretation of living in the light.

Notice the Light

Notice the light in the foggy morning haze that whispers common secrets into the breaking dawn.

Notice the light in steps taken over roots and around pebbles, over logs and through icy rain.

Notice the light in the leaves of seasons now past as they surrender into a path for whomever needs one.

Notice the light in ancient boulders that sit, watching, with emerald moss and sea green lichens as their constant companions.

Notice the light in rushing torrents of spring that churn and thunder down ravines that ache to come fully into life.

Notice the light in melancholy, in the moods that we don't want and in the space that is held for such contrast.

Notice the light that persists through impermanence.

Acquiesce

Spring came early this year to the Midwest. Last week the overnight lows bottomed out at -11 and the world was still bright white after a fresh snowfall at the end of February and the ground rock solid. This week the highs are singing themselves into the 60s, the world is brown once more, and the earth gives again under our weight. There are a few memories of white left deep in the forest and behind the biggest boulders in the ravine, but most traces of winter have melted away. The seasonal stream has run and dried up, within the same week. The lake is still a swath of ice, and will be for a while yet, but the geese have returned and the trumpeter swans that wintered at the place where the river doesn't freeze are calling out a welcome. Just like the fall that suddenly turned to winter with a foot of snow and plummeting temperatures, the season has now suddenly turned to spring under a powerful March sun and snow that was quick to surrender to its urgency.

I've been reading a lot about vulnerability, and the challenges we humans have when it comes to embracing such a state, in the last few weeks. It seems like good timing, as the season changes. The natural world doesn't struggle with putting itself out there and being vulnerable. It just does it because there is no other option. A flower comes up in the spring and offers itself to the elements, whatever they turn out to be. A tree buds when warm enough temperatures invite it to do so, even if there's a hard freeze looming—it doesn't hesitate, or worry about what might happen, or hide behind a fear of what might come next. Presenting new life unfolding is the only choice. Even if it means getting frozen as a result.

Brene Brown writes, "There's nothing more daring than showing up, putting ourselves out there and letting ourselves be seen."

Like the flower that buds just in time for a late spring snowfall, or the apple tree that gives up its autumn fruit for the chance to bud with the first warmth after winter, we can let our beauty be seen when we step out into the sun. We might fall, we might get covered up by snow, we might freeze to the ground and have to ask for help. We will surely be uncomfortable, and we will probably be afraid of what might come next. But we will be courageous and we will be living in the only place that allows us to be fully alive.

So spring may have come early to Minnesota, and we wonder what that will mean for the upcoming growing season and the world in general as the climate continues to shift. But we can use the vulnerabilities of nature to hold onto the remembrance of what it means to dare to live without apologies and full of self-worth and gratitude for the chance to be seen.

Everyday Contentment

Eva's birthday is in March. And as she grows and learns and astonishes us with each new milestone, I have noticed myself reflecting more and more on the first few months of her life. She arrived on a Sunday morning as winter gave way to spring, full of life and ready to embrace her humanness as only a brand new human can. There was snow lingering on the ground, and the sunrise that day was full of anticipation and the unknowing that comes along with waiting for something that is impossible to predict.

We brought her home a few days later, unsure and anxious as so many new parents are, and settled into a rhythm that was punctuated with nursing, changing diapers, washing diapers, bouncing the baby to sleep, and waiting for her to cry so the pattern could continue. It was a rhythm of trial and melancholy and immeasurable joy, somehow all rolled into one. As the cliché goes, having a baby changes everything.

I remember the first day I left the house alone to walk around a nearby lake. I remember feeling anxious that she would need to nurse while I was gone and that my husband would have to deal with a screeching infant until my return. I remember stepping around melting piles of grey snow and skirting mud puddles as I made my way down the driveway, out to the gravel road. I remember feeling the sun on my face and how good it felt to reclaim the use of my physical body.

I remember feeling like that walk—even with the mud puddles and drab weather—was enough to satisfy my need to feel alive and in my own skin, one human embracing her humanness, for the rest of the day. I remember coming back into the house and melting back into the rhythm. I remember feeling like just being part of that rhythm was enough.

That feeling of contentment from having just one half hour alone, outside, moving over the earth on foot lasted for several months. I felt a sense of peace after coming in from a run, or time spent in the garden, or the occasional longer hike in the woods.

I went back to work full-time and started running or gardening in the morning as the sun came up. Despite the extra demands that came with adding work to the rhythm of the days, that sense of peace—the sense that the ordinary rhythm of 'life with baby' was enough—lingered. For a while.

A few months after Eva marked her first birthday, I noticed that sense of peace slipping. I found myself wanting more time, more resources, and more flexibility to do what I wanted to do.

I found myself wanting to feel like I was making a difference, like I mattered enough, like I was *enjoying* enough. I found myself *wanting* to feel content with life and wanting to feel satisfied with the everyday. But I wasn't.

Somewhere in the space between my daughter's birth and her twenty month birthday, that sense of peace got stuck behind a different rhythm that felt busy and lacking and not enough. A half-hour walk outside wasn't doing it for me anymore. After coming inside, I wanted another half hour, and then another, and then another. Sometimes all the time in the world, all the recognition in the world, all the happiness in the world... it didn't feel like enough.

I can't say that I have completely regained that feeling of complete contentment. But as I reflect on the months just after my daughter's birth, I reclaim some of that peace. In acknowledging that feeling of lack, of discontent, and of happiness that comes and goes, I am inviting that peace to return to the rhythm.

It will undoubtedly still be a rhythm of trial, of melancholy, and of immeasurable joy, because that is what being human is about. It is about celebrating the mountaintops and accepting the valleys and their shadows.

It is about remembering that joy and peace remain present even when they seem buried beneath wanting, discontent and overwhelming schedules. It is about seeing the extraordinary in something as mundane as a walk around a frozen lake on a muddy gravel road. It is about remembering that we are all full of life and have the capacity to fully embrace our humanness.

It is about recognizing the instinct to do something to change a feeling or the persistent need to address our desire for more—and letting it be there. Sometimes there's simply nothing to do but accept that being human means letting all feelings speak, and then letting them pass when they no longer serve.

Perhaps embracing our humanness and the life that comes with it means celebrating the anticipation and the unknowing that comes with waiting for something that is impossible to predict.

The Invisible Thread

There's a thread you follow. It goes among
things that change. But it doesn't change.
People wonder about what you are pursuing.
You have to explain about the thread.
—William Stafford

The first person I called after four weeks of training to be a corporate health coach was a gentleman who I'll call Charlie. The appointment was at 7PM on a Tuesday in early April, and I had literally all day to prepare and worry about how it would go. When the witching hour finally rolled around, I dialed the phone, had my paper at the ready to take notes and half hoped that he wouldn't answer. But he did answer, and at the end of the conversation, he had a goal to play basketball once a week and eat one less serving of pasta when spaghetti was on the table for dinner. And I knew that he had a six year old daughter going through treatment for leukemia and that he felt powerless in the face of something so important that was outside of his control. In twenty minutes I learned what made this person who I'd probably never meet get up in the morning and what drove him to take care of himself. I learned about some of his challenges, and I learned of his struggles to stay on track. I asked him what his vision of a healthy life was, and he told me it was to be his best self so he could give his daughter the dad she deserved. Most of his story I'll never know, and he didn't have to tell me the parts that he did. But he chose to share, and I chose to listen, and now our stories will forever be intertwined.

I came to health coaching on a whim—it was one possibility out of many after completing graduate school. One morning as winter lingered and the city that was home at the time sighed under the weight of snow that wanted to melt but couldn't yet, I showed up to an interview with the manager of a new health coaching department at a growing health management company. I answered the interview questions, faked my way through a role play and left with a job. I figured I'd last a year or two and then move onto the next thing. After all, health coaching? What was that anyway? I had no idea what I was doing. And I didn't really want to sit at a desk in a cubicle talking to people on the phone all day.

That spring was years ago and I now live well outside the city limits and work from a home office. I still don't always feel like I know what I'm doing, but most of the time I do pretty well, at least according to my performance reviews. Interacting with real people is unpredictable and messy, no matter where your home base is and no matter how long you've been doing a job. But despite the challenges, there is something powerful and real about what goes on during my work days. I can't say I love the phone time, or the centrality of the computer to the work that I do, or the fast pace at which the corporation I work for grows, but these years working as a coach have provided a springboard into possibilities that didn't exist before I took the chance to do something that felt like it was outside my comfort zone. Talking to relative strangers all day isn't usually a job that has introverted people lining up at the door, excited to begin. But doing so has forced me to hold on tight to the invisible thread that guides me when I remember it's there. I certainly don't always remember it's there. But when I can feel the thread, and when I remember that authentic connection, both to other humans and to nature, has to be the cornerstone from which I operate at the office, it makes a difference. I have to remember to keep it real.

Mary Oliver writes, "Do you think there is anything not attached by its unbreakable cord to everything else?"

When I hold onto my thread, that unbreakable cord that binds me to all the things of the world—both human and non-human—I can remember that my work allows me to weave into the tapestry of someone else's story, and then out again, as the story of what it means to be on earth unfolds.

Tap into the Earth's Intelligence

Spring has arrived here in Minnesota. Though the trees remain bare and the ground is still mostly brown, there is a fresh resonance outside—there's an energy to the ground when you walk that wasn't there just a few weeks ago. The frost has moved up and out, and the soil is regaining warmth. The moss on the shady hillsides is starting to come to life with new delicate light-green growth, and the silver maple trees are starting to bud. Things are waking up. Birdsong fills the air from dawn to dusk, I can hear the newest members of the beaver family barking to each other as they learn the lay of the lake, and the ice-free water sparkles with every breeze that ruffles its surface. I can sense the re-forging of winter dormant connections as the days progress and the sun regains power.

In my day job as a health coach, I talk to all sorts of people who work for large companies around the country. I talk to linemen who work in oil fields, coal miners, executives, salespeople, secretaries, teachers, call center workers, managers, nurses, even the occasional big AG farmer or chemist....there are a lot of jobs and professions that are controlled by the corporate world today. And as I talk with this wide range of people, the theme that comes out is that there is not enough time for, well, anything and spending time outside in a natural setting is either a luxury for the weekend or something to be avoided unless it is sunny and 78 degrees. Even many of the farmers spend a fair amount of their time inside—or in the cab of a climate controlled piece of machinery. People are generally stressed out, have too much going on and spend most of their time working on their daily tasks indoors or commuting to the places where they need to be. Of course, there are exceptions to this generalization and not every person who works for a corporation fits into this description. But overall, I have witnessed a huge disconnect in corporate culture between people and the natural environment.

The problems with this disconnect are many, but the one that I want to focus on is that due to this "people as separate" approach to life and the ways that we literally disconnect our physical bodies from the bare earth, we are setting ourselves up for lowered immunity, increased inflammation in the body, and a less than desirable sense of wellbeing.

According to Dr. James Oschman, "we have disconnected ourselves from the Earth by putting rubber and plastic on the bottoms of our shoes."

Due to our indoor lifestyle and the perceived need to protect ourselves from natural elements, whether it is by wearing sturdy shoes at all times, living in concrete jungles or just being afraid to get dirty, we hinder our ability to ground ourselves and benefit from the freely given energy of the earth.

Oschman writes, "When you're grounded there's a transfer of free electrons from the Earth into your body. And these free electrons are probably some of the most potent antioxidants known to man. These antioxidants are responsible for things like beneficial changes in heart rate, decreased skin resistance and decreased levels of inflammation as observed in clinical studies."

A few weeks ago, just after the last of the snow melted away and the ground became spongy again, I walked outside barefoot onto the mossy ground that covers much of my front yard. The earth was still cold to the touch and damp in these first weeks of spring, but it was warm enough to stand for a while on a little piece of moss and feel the rootedness that comes from such direct contact with the earth. I could feel my body relaxing into the more primal rhythms of the season, and I could feel the power of such a connection wake something up in my system that had gone to sleep in the depths of winter. I could feel into my place on the earth and the potential that a simple act can have toward the healing of the planet and all the communities that exist here.

Hema Simondes writes, "Unlike all other species ever to have lived on this planet, it seems that overall the human race has lost its way, our essential connection to this paradise [of earth], and our ability to live sustainably. We often forget or ignore that it's only by this grace and generosity of the Earth, our original and true mother, that we may sustain this physical life at all. Our survival as a species is intimately linked to a healthy relationship with our environment."

Based on all I've read and experienced, the message is this: We need to go barefoot on the earth, at least sometimes. We need to be in direct physical contact with this planet that provides a foundation from which to live. Whether it's standing outside on the lawn, walking through a forest or a grassy field, laying on the sand at the beach or wading in a creek, the options are many. And the benefits are beyond what we can imagine. Like Rainer Maria Rilke says, "If we surrendered to the earth's intelligence, we could rise up rooted, like trees."

Shopping With Integrity

It's fair to say I dread most things about visiting my local big box grocery store: from driving to its location perched just off the highway to piloting the car (and a car's a must...these establishments are typically not pedestrian friendly) through the football field sized parking lot to dodging traffic on foot to get to the front doors to navigating a cart through aisle after aisle of brightly colored packages, searching in vain for something that fits with my family's organic, non-processed food preferences and then scanning what I do find through the automated check-out line while the people behind me wait impatiently because my apples are rolling around because I don't like to put them in the plastic bags the store provides. In short, it's stressful, over stimulating and isolating all rolled into one "convenient" experience. I typically leave big chain stores feeling depleted even though the goal upon entering was to procure some nourishing, life sustaining food. I leave feeling like a consumer; like just another one of the numbers on an economic checklist.

Last Sunday I had a few unexpected hours to myself in the afternoon, so I figured I'd use the time to get some things done that are easier to do without a toddler in tow. I needed some flour, some broccoli (our toddler's veggie of choice these days) and some cream. I needed to clean the bathroom, do the laundry and bring in some firewood. I thought about heading to the local chain store on my way home from dropping Eva off at her grandparents'—it is right on the way and the act of going in to purchase a couple items would have been a quick detour. It would have been over and done in 15 minutes, and I would have been on my way to the next thing on my list.

But I didn't. Instead, I drove a little out of my way, over the river and through the downtown area of St. Croix Falls, WI, a little town that's partially perched on the riverbanks of the St. Croix River. I drove just a touch north of town to the Wert Nature Preserve (450 beautiful acres that have been dedicated to providing space for creatures to thrive and humans to visit by treading lightly and respecting the natural state of the area) and poked around on the newly melted trails. The errand list, well, that could wait. Somehow the choice to avoid the pull of a house in need of cleaning and the convenience of an enormous parking lot plus some shiny pre-packaged goods inspired me to head to the woods instead. There was water running in the creek beds, but due to low snow levels this past winter, it was dry enough to hike around on the trails that wind up the hillsides. I meandered around for a few miles, reveled in the strangely warm March air and made a point to notice the sounds and textures of which I was immersed. Since I did still need flour, broccoli and cream, I took one final deep breath of the forest air and made my way back into town.

And instead of driving up the hill to the local big box chain that has everything one could possibly need within the same four walls, I went to Fine Acres Market. Situated in the midst of a quaint downtown stretch of mostly local businesses, there's only street parking, and I usually have to walk a ways from where I find a spot. It's a small shop, with just enough room for bulk bins of things like flour, spices, and other grains, another for supplements and body care, and an area for dairy and produce. It's encouraged to bring your own bags, and I also try to remember to return the glass milk bottles that the local organic dairy uses. It takes a little extra time to wash my hands and scoop flour, assemble the other bulk items in the array of used bags that I have stashed at the bottom of various canvas totes and write down the prices for the cashier. Sometimes I don't find every single thing on my list. After all, a store that likes to source things locally just isn't always going to have broccoli in March. (But they did this time!) But everything is organic. I get to choose how much I want. Many of the goods come from someplace close by. And there's always a kind person working the till, happy to answer questions or just chat about the day. In short, the feeling of the place is life-giving and sustaining. It's not stressful, and I always find myself lingering. I leave the store feeling uplifted and good about my place in the world. I leave feeling like I was just part of a positive exchange of energy instead of just another economic transaction that feeds an unsustainable system.

So my errands on this unexpectedly free afternoon took longer than anticipated, and I didn't get everything on my to-do list done as a result. But at the end of the day I felt like a complete person. I could have spent the afternoon buying convenience and time, but instead I chose to use that time to be an intentional part of the aspects of my community that truly align with what I value most. Do I always make that choice? No. I wish I did, but sometimes ease and hurry get the best of me. But every time I do choose intentionality over convenience? Well, I guess I'm just that much closer to my wish. I suppose then I'm shopping with integrity.

Value

I see value in the eight week old chickens that spend their days poking around in the sparse woods, climbing logs and honing their scratching skills in the spring soil as their caretakers commit themselves to making a new way of life. I see value in the neighbor's greeting as he gathers the last buckets of a maple's sweet life blood at the close of this year's sap run and in the children who offer their enthusiasm to the project. I see value in new trees being planted, in spring snow giving way to spring sun, and in the hints of green that cast a hue of promise over the fields. I see value in the wood duck perched high in the basswood tree, in the gentle flap of a sandhill crane's wings overhead, and in the beaver, the keeper of the lake. I see value in life unfolding organically all around me.

It turns out that the value needed to sustain abundant life isn't found in a bank, a trust fund, or a gold bar. Value isn't in the numbers of a dollar amount next to the numbers of a checking account when I look at my online banking profile. Value doesn't come from putting in overtime for a company that works for profit of a few.

Real value can be found in the sacred of life, in the people and creatures that call the earth home, and in the energy exchange that flows between everything in the universe.

There is a Native American saying which goes something like this: "Only when the last tree has withered, the last fish has been caught, and the last river has been poisoned, will we realize we cannot eat money."

No one wants this to be the end of our story: Not the linemen who work for oil companies. Not the suburbanites who drive army vehicles to get their groceries at the nearest Walmart. Not the farmer who sprays his GMO crops with Roundup. Not the commuter who travels two hours every day to get to a high paying trading job on Wall Street.

We need to remember where our value lies, and use it. We need to remember that the reason we are alive and in communion with this place, this earth, is to experience the abundance that is possible when we allow it in. We need to judge less and love more. We need to cling to the outcome we want less and accept more. We need to turn a blind eye to the cry of the earth less and listen more. We need to see value where the value is.

Earth Day in a New Story

Daniel Quinn, author of the book *Ishmael,* writes that, "There's nothing fundamentally wrong with people. Given a story to enact that puts them in accord with the world, they will live in accord with the world. But given a story to enact that puts them at odds with the world, as yours does, they will live at odds with the world." Mr. Quinn sheds light on a lot of interesting things about our culture that we don't see on the surface, or at least things that we don't let ourselves acknowledge much of the time. You might say that the story we are in right now is one that sees the earth as a resource—a thing to be used—complete with a hierarchy of power with the richest of humans at the very top. You might say, as Llewellyn Vaughan-Lee does, that, "We are the inheritors of this culture [story] that has banished the relationship to the sacred from the Earth."

Yet even if we know all there is to know about how stuck we are in this story, we are still stuck. I know that burning fuel oil to heat the house is only harming the earth in many ways, yet today we filled the tank because we ran out after a really long, cold winter, and with a baby in the house, we are not OK with just leaving the heat off. We want to put in a wood stove and get our electrical power from solar panels, but those things take money to acquire and time to put in, and we did not have either of those things today. We need heat right now. So we had to fill the tank. Even though we know what we know.

I find myself being resistant to spending money on big ticket items like solar panels and wood stoves, yet when we run out of fuel oil, I don't hesitate to hand over the cash to pay for it. Because we had to, or we'd be in a cold house until spring decides to show up for the year. How do we get to the place where we do things that fit with what we know, instead of just reacting to the old patterns that we wish were different?

Today, April 22ND, is Earth Day. To be fair, I'm glad the current story has an Earth Day. But I want to be in a new story that doesn't celebrate Earth Day—because the characters in the new one don't need a reminder to live as one with the whole of the earth. How do we shift our thinking into an awareness that breaks free from our conditioning and our fear of doing things in a radically different way? How do we tell a new story?

Much of the time, I have no idea. Or I have ideas but too much fear to act on them in full. Or I come up with some kind of plan to do things differently, and then get distracted by the everydayness of life. Or I forget that every failure has the potential to be a foundation for success, eventually, if I would only see them as stepping stones instead of black holes.

But maybe, when we recognize that we are in a story that doesn't end well, we can take action to change it. It won't happen rapidly, even though that would be ideal. It will surely take planning and doing things that make us feel uncomfortable and stretch what we feel we have the capacity to undertake. It will likely be frustrating since many people around us will want to remain totally invested in the old story and unable or unwilling to listen to the new one that is finding its voice through us.

Quinn goes on to say, "Once you learn to discern the voice of Mother Culture humming in the background, telling her story over and over again to the people of your culture, you'll never stop being conscious of it. Wherever you go for the rest of your life, you'll be tempted to say to the people around you, 'how can you listen to this stuff and not recognize it for what it is?'"

Can two stories live side by side if some people choose not to recognize the illusion of the broken one they have been in for so long? Maybe they can for a while. I am inclined to think that the old story has to fade away for the new one to continue and thrive. For the earth to regain wholeness and vibrancy, we need to see with new eyes and remember the sacred in ourselves that *is* the earth. Then maybe we can get unstuck and into a new story—one that sets people up to live in accord with the world.

Be the Water

As I go about my office work days, my body rebels against sitting at a computer station in the form of a sore back and a right arm that feels slightly disconnected from how it should. I would rather be sore from chopping wood or planting an acre of kale by hand. I am reminded of how far away from our roots we have gotten as a human species—and how much we need to remember those roots.

We click away on computer keyboards and scroll through information on touch screens hour after hour, day after day. There are good things about technology, to be sure. We can stay connected and get information more easily than ever before. But we also lose something if we let technology take the reins—when we let it dictate our choices and our day-to-day actions. We read about nature online instead of taking time to walk in the woods, we send emails in greeting instead of knocking on a door, we listen to recordings of soothing nature sounds to relax instead of opening the windows, and we look up weather conditions on a news website instead of stepping out the front door to experience them in full. We watch television or play video games instead of having conversations or living our own adventure. How strange we must look to other creatures.

Do we notice that our behavior has gotten so out of touch with reality that we destroy the elements that keep us alive?

Some of us do. Some of us who notice keep living like we always have. Some of us are preoccupied. Some of us want to rule the world. I wonder what it will take for us to get back in touch with the part of ourselves that IS nature, the part that yearns to see its unique weave in the tapestry of creation. I wonder if I notice my weave enough. I wonder if noticing can heal what's broken or unbalanced. I wonder how I can take the noticing and use it to live in a way that is truly woven deep into the soil that nourishes, into the air that breathes, and into the water that keeps intention flowing into being.

I wonder how to remember to be the water.

I can hear birds chirping and frogs singing to each other this morning. Life outside is in full swing as creatures of all sorts revel in the newly warm temperatures and in celebration that everything is waking up with the arrival of a new season. There are seed potatoes sprouting in a box by my feet, waiting to be planted and broccoli seedlings outside the door getting used to the natural air before moving to their soil bed in the garden. Wildflowers of brilliant blue and bright white are popping up through old leaf cover in the woods, and the great blue heron has made his homecoming to the shores of the lake. After a winter that was punctuated with more snow and more cold later than we wanted, spring has embraced the landscape again.

Despite the seemingly constant hum of industrial progress, and the drone of lack and longing that rides a fine line between illusion and reality, the essence of the earth persists at casting shadows of joy all around us. If we look closely, we can see the weaves that connect everything, and the rhythm. And we can see the light that radiates when each piece of creation's mystery adds a note to the hymn that is being written.

Woven Deep

The care of the Earth is our most ancient and most
worthy, and after all our most pleasing responsibility.
To cherish what remains of it and to foster its
renewal is our only hope.
—WENDELL BERRY

This past Sunday afternoon my husband Nick, my brother Andrew, his partner, and I did our first walk around the land that we are set to purchase next Tuesday morning. The experience was simple enough: We scouted out where to plow up a patch for veggies, thought about where to place a shelter belt of trees and visualized how berry bushes would look on the hillside. We shoveled soil into clean plastic bags from a few sites to see what additional nutrients it might need to support vegetable or fruit plants. We poked around in the wooded area that leads down to the lake, noting signs of deer and spring weeds coming back to life after winter.

This land that happens to be next door to our current property came up for sale last summer, just a year after we moved to the area, and we have all been toying with the idea of trying to buy it off and on since then. In recent months, those thoughts have turned into actions, and we have ironed out the details enough to plunk down the cash needed to call it our own. So though this land idea has been swirling around for over half a year now, it was a rather profound experience to look at the area with this new perspective and put voice to goals that will help our still evolving vision move forward.

The most recent idea is to turn this modest 5 acres (almost 10 if you count the land we already own) into a biodynamic garden. Biodynamic farming principles are not new—these principles actually predate the use of "organic" to describe growing practices and methods. According to the world's only certification organization of biodynamic farms and products, Demeter-usa branch:

> Biodynamic farming is a holistic and regenerative farm-ing system that is focused on soil health, the integration of plants and animals, and biodiversity. It seeks to create a farm system that is minimally dependant on imported materials, and instead meets its needs from the living dynamics of the farm itself. It is the biodiversity of the farm, organized so that the waste of one part of the farm becomes the energy for another, that results in an increase in the farm's capacity for self-renewal and ultimately makes the farm sustainable.

Reaching certification would take some time and a lot of very hard work, but it is an exciting prospect to work toward. As we begin to till up the hay that resides in the fields now and replace it with organic matter and seedlings, we will inch closer to de-veloping a section of land into a place that will support abun-dant life, nourish the community and promote holistic health. If that's not worth a lot of hard work, I don't know what is. Care of our physical bodies, of each other and of the earth are all woven deeply together. Everything is connected. Everything is woven deep.

Walk in Beauty

This year April is coming to a close through a chilly haze punctuated by rain and soggy ground and more rain. Though we have some seedlings thriving under grow lights in the house, the field and garden beds have yet to be prepared, and nothing has been planted outside yet, unless you count the rhubarb that I moved to a new location over the weekend. I am itching to get some seeds in the ground....and I imagine the carrot, pea, bean, lettuce, beet and radish seeds are getting a little stir crazy in their storage pouches. After a winter that lingered, I am ready to dig into the newly warmed soil and nurture the growth that will provide sustenance in the year to come.

Back in March, I met up with some fellow gardening neighbors for a seed swap, and one of those neighbors offered us the use of their 18/8 foot greenhouse. Their land can't accommodate its need to sit flat, so they graciously invited us to provide it a home and use it for the upcoming growing season. While an exciting prospect, now comes the challenge of figuring out how to move an 18/8 foot greenhouse down a mile of gravel road to its new home in our field. The rain doesn't look to be letting up anytime soon, so we have some time to ponder our options. Silver lining, I suppose.

While the chilly haze lingers and the rain washes new gullies into being and re-fills the lakes after years of too little moisture, we look ahead to the long, hot days of summer and visualize big red tomatoes and shiny cucumbers and bright yellow peppers enjoying the heat of a gifted greenhouse. We gaze at the seedlings inching higher each day under their grow lights and witness their slow progression toward fullness and marvel at their unfolding beauty. We see the rain through a lens of gratitude for the way it nourishes the earth and provides the contrast—the rest—that we need to move joyfully through our days.

And as the sun sets on another rainy day in Minnesota, through the mist I can see the youthful leaves of the ash tree dance in the moisture, and the last of the bloodroot flowers are folding up their petals for the evening. Though spring is getting a slow start, the world is slowly starting to take on tints of green, the frogs have taken up their singing in full and birdsong fills the air at all hours of the day. We have harvested wild ramps and nettles and relish in the first truly fresh tastes of the year. The beauty of new life is springing up all around us, and even the quiet nights are humming with the prospect of abundance and growth.

Soon the onions will be planted, the garlic will be 5 inches high and the big field will be warm enough for tomato seedlings and squash seeds. The resident woodchuck will put forth a solid effort to devour the tender pepper and kale seedlings that will be set out to harden off outside in the back, and the potatoes will enjoy nestling into their new home in the spring soil.

All of life is gathering silent strength for the growing season ahead, and we give thanks for the generosity and kindness of others as we commit to spreading that generosity and kindness wider with each action that we take and with each seed that we sow.

The Antidote

Here's a summary of what's been going on in the last two weeks: Both of the family cars have needed repair, I had to commute to the city in pouring rain in one of those cars (that was still broken at the time) to spend a workday at a corporate office, the weather insists on remaining cold and damp enough to make the furnace kick in regularly, property taxes and student loans are due, my spouse is beyond busy with projects, and the garden weeds already need attention. And then the fridge broke. Modern life—when you don't live in a metro area full of good take out options—is more challenging without a refrigerator.

Yesterday as I was washing the dishes, reflecting on (agonizing over) all of the things that have happened over the last few weeks (as my husband took apart the freezer in an attempt to fix the fridge while our two year old sang/yelled at the top of her lungs as she ran around in the middle of the kitchen), I got to that overwhelmed place that we all get to sometimes when so many things start piling up. And then I started giggling. I'm not really much of a giggler, usually. The giggling wasn't very far removed from sobbing, I'm sure, but instead of misery, my life situation apparently wanted a more light hearted coping technique. In that moment while my hands were covered in soap bubbles, anyway.

Oliver Burkeman writes in his book titled *The Antidote*: "[Research] points to an alternative approach, a 'negative path' to happiness that entails taking a radically different stance towards those things most of us spend our lives trying hard to avoid. This involves learning to enjoy uncertainty, embracing insecurity and becoming familiar with failure. In order to be truly happy, it turns out, we might actually need to be willing to experience more negative emotions—or, at the very least, to stop running quite so hard from them."

While putting some of those dishes away and dodging the small body that was darting around the kitchen over discarded fridge parts, it occurred to me that despite the less than ideal circumstances that have punctuated life lately, I could still breathe through the tints of negativity. I could still stand at the sink and let the uncertainty of life be uncertain, and I could still find joy in the midst of a broken refrigerator. Happiness is still possible in tandem with jobs that want energy that sometimes isn't there for the taking and with external events that we wouldn't wish on anyone else.

Burkeman goes on to write, "It turns out that there's a long tradition in philosophy and spirituality that's about embracing negativity, about easing up on all of this positive thinking and learning instead to bathe in insecurity, uncertainty and failure, and to find the enormous potential for happiness that's lurking inside all that."

Though I look forward to the day when the kitchen is back in working order, the cars are running perfectly, my child prefers reading quietly to yelling, and I am sitting on the sun-bathed back deck instead of in my office, I can find a semblance of contentment in knowing that all circumstances and the feelings that follow are a part of the whole. I can remind myself that it is, after all, simply the beliefs that I hold about my life situation that color the events as good or bad. Without those beliefs, they just are. And when they just exist—without a label—giggling at the sink when life threatens to overwhelm transforms my experience of living in that chaos and invites enough tranquility to overshadow despair. Perhaps when we let our experiences—all of them—be what they are, we are more apt to finally see the joy that is lurking just outside of our sightlines.

The Transformation of Loss

Minnesota is welcoming the later part of spring this year with warm temperatures, very little rain and lots of sunshine. The lake down the hill is being swallowed up by weeds already, but the birds and frogs are conversing, the wildflowers are holding up their brightly colored arms in triumph, Jack in the Pulpit has returned to the shady parts of the woods and the crab apple trees are flaunting their beauty as only a flowering apple tree can. And today brings the rains and the earth drinks up the nourishment like a tonic. Life is emerging and flowing and thriving in every direction, and it shows no sign of letting up.

But in the midst of all this growth and aliveness, there are abrupt endings and death, too. A river that flows in a nearby state claimed a young life over a weekend, and a family in my community mourns a son. A few weeks ago, the river that flows a few miles from my house claimed someone's daughter. A dear friend lost her brother a few days ago and may never know why. Cancer took a friend of a friend sooner than anyone thought it would. The sweet spring air is laced with a sense of loss, and it is jarring to try to find one's balance as the beauty and vibrancy of a new season sits next to the sadness and grief of death.

Anne Lamott writes, in *Stitches: A Handbook on Meaning, Hope and Repair,* "One rarely knows where to begin the search for meaning, though by necessity, we can only start where we are... It somehow has to do with sticking together as we try to make sense of chaos, and that seems a way to begin.

We try to help where we can, and try to survive our own trials and stresses, illnesses and elections. We work really hard at not being driven crazy by noise and speed and extremely annoying people, whose names we are too polite to mention. We try not to be tripped up by major global sadness, difficulties in our families or the death of [those dear to us]...

We work hard, we enjoy life as best we can, we endure. We try to help ourselves and one another. We try to be more present and less petty. Some days go better than others. We look for solace in nature and art and maybe, if we are lucky, the quiet satisfaction of our homes."

We work hard, we try to enjoy life, we endure. Life so many times is harder than we want it to be. "It's just the human condition," they say. Maybe they are right. Maybe we humans are inevitably drawn into chaos, turmoil and bleak moods just because it's the human condition. We seem to invite destruction into our habitat and each other and ourselves more every day. We let systems keep us captive, we give in to convenience, and we let fatigue overshadow our values. We don't know how to ask for help, or give of ourselves, much of the time. We have a hard time finding meaning in our day to day actions, and we are stuck in the past or worrying about the future. Sometimes the present feels too painful to greet head on. The world churns and we get lost in the global maladies of our time. We get lost in our own grief, and we get lost in the grief of others. We don't know the answers and we forget to look at the sky.

This week I feel for the ones who lost those dear to them in unexpected ways. I wonder how to give my support, and many times I am unsure of what to say. I suspect that simply showing up and feeling the enormity of what has happened is what is important, but no one has a road map for navigating something that has never happened before. Every death, every tragedy, is new; never to be repeated. Like every birth, every blossoming, every newly unfurled leaf, death leaves us gasping in astonishment. It leaves us searching for meaning under what happened. It shows us the amazement of life, and it shows us the fragility. It offers these things to us as another's life passes on into whatever comes next.

It can feel like we live in a system built on hopeless chaos, yet there is good news in our midst. Sometimes wildflowers fill the highway ditches and the scent of newly uncovered pine needles filters through the sweet air to remind us that we are here, now. We may be stuck in despair and searching for meaning in things that are swirling around us, never to be pinned down...but we will once again see the beauty in the churning energy that flows and glues together life and death on this earth. We will see beyond the broken tea cups and the crushed blossoms and the hopes that will never be fulfilled in a human lifetime because we have the capacity to see the solace that exists in each moment as it unfolds—when we notice the grace of life that underlies everything.

Lamott goes on to say, "It can be healthy to hate what life has given you, and to insist on being a big mess for a while. This takes great courage. But then, at some point, the better of two choices is to get back up on your feet and live again."

Just as there is unfathomable beauty in life, so too is there agony, pain and suffering. And just as there is unfathomable agony, pain and suffering tied to death, so too are there hints of life's beauty. Not a beauty that those who are close to the ones who have passed can see in the moments, days or months of raw grief, but perhaps rather a beauty that emerges as a life, no matter how long, is celebrated. It comes out, perhaps, in a community that comes together to support each other in the midst of heartache. It comes out, perhaps, when we can remember that a human life is much bigger than a bodily human death.

Meghan O'Rourke writes, "It's not a question of getting over it or healing. No; it's a question of learning to live with this transformation. For the loss is transformative, in good ways and bad. It's a tangle of change that cannot be threaded into the usual narrative spools. It is too central for that. It's not an emergence from the cocoon, but a tree growing around an obstruction."

Perhaps the beauty comes out in the transformation that happens whether we want it to or not. Maybe the transformation is enough.

Dance in Jubilation

May Day is a day that I remember celebrating in primary school by making a basket filled with paper flowers to give to my mother. I can recall giving it to her out in our backyard while standing next to the flowering lilac bush. In the memory, the lilacs are filling the air with their sweet smell, and purple petals are raining down on us as we twirl in frothy white dresses amidst a sea of silky grass and the last of the tulips…. but I think in the 30 years that have passed since the event, May Day and Mother's Day got rolled into one, along with a little bit of a dream on the side. At any rate, the first day of May is a time to celebrate, give of ourselves and take deep breaths of air laced with the sweet scent of spring blossoming.

In Irish mythology, May Day is known as Beltane—a time when the door to winter is firmly shut as the season of summer and lushness waits in the wings. But it isn't here yet—this time of mid spring is a time of planting seeds, of transformation, of emergence and of reclaiming the communities that we let go dormant when the days got dark. But the light is back, and earth is green, and the soil is aching to support new life.

Today Eva and I spent most of the afternoon meandering around in the woods near our home looking for Jack in the Pulpit, wandering through the hay field looking for fairies and examining gopher holes, and speculating when Jerry, the neighbor who graciously tills up part of our garden each year, would arrive to do the deed. We discovered a new egg in the ground sparrow nest that we'd found the day before, danced around clutching dandelions and last year's Black eyed Susans and after a while, marveled at the smell of freshly turned over soil as Eva cheered the tiller on as only a four year old can.

But back to the old traditions. One of the ancient Beltane customs was to douse the fire in the home hearth that had been burning all winter long and start one anew, this time lighting the home hearth from the community bonfire as a way to rekindle connections and share energy with neighbors.

We didn't light a community bonfire today, and our home hearth has been doused for weeks already. But we did refresh conversations that were left off back in the fall. We didn't jump over burning embers to encourage fertility, but we did jump in jubilation upon seeing new life spring forth from the ground and from other creatures around us. We didn't dance around a May pole, but we did engage in the ancient yet always new dance that is given rhythm by the turn of the year.

May Day here wasn't anything that may have appeared out of the ordinary, but in the midst of just another spring day, we welcomed the transformation and revitalization that happens when we let the earth lead.

Goodness
through Discomfort

May this year ended with a flood, literally, as 5 inches of rain in a few hours identified the path of least resistance to be one that led into the crawl space where the well pump comes into the basement. After a soggy spring, all that water finally wanted some time inside to dry off. We bailed the water with an old ice cream pail, stretched out sore backs from too much crouching in small spaces and hung the old wet towels in the utility sink to drip at their leisure. When the sun came back out, we went outside to see how the rest of the area fared after the storms.

Despite the inconvenience of water where we don't want it, all of the rain has given the newly planted tomatoes, peppers, squash, melons, chard, strawberries and Brussels sprouts the moisture they crave as they dig their roots into new homes of field soil and lay claim to abundant growth in the months ahead. The older strawberry plants and blueberry bushes are bigger than ever and full of little white flowers that can't wait to turn into berries. The garlic that was planted last fall is knee high and thinks more and more about sending scapes skyward with each passing day. Apple and cherry blossoms have come and gone, and the asparagus continues to send out new shoots. And the shoots we let grow rapidly contribute to a developing forest, despite the persistence of a small asparagus beetle army. There are Indian corn infants and canna bulbs, gifted from some neighbors, starting to poke through the ebony soil, and Grandma K's lilies are vibrant green and more abundant than ever. The lake is full to the brim and the air is constantly humming with birds and frogs telling their stories and marking this space as theirs to share.

Spring is coming to a close with soggy ground and soiled towels, threats of mold and the need for more mulch. We humans find discomfort in the inconvenience of too much rain all at once, and the plants simply let it fall and drink up the goodness it can leave behind. The earth gives thanks for the cycles and helps us to remember why we chose this way of life, and what it can bring when we notice the goodness that is possible.

Mother Superior

Though its waters are fresh and crystal,
superior is a sea. It breeds storms and rains and fogs,
like a sea. It is cold in mid-summer as the Atlantic.
It is wild, and masterful.
—GEORGE GRANT

Lake Superior makes her home on the earth about 120 miles northeast of my little red house in the St. Croix River Valley. She's vast, cold and clear, and without a bit of time spent on her shores regularly I get a little twitchy. There's something about the volume of deep fresh water that can refresh even the weariest of souls and balance whatever needs balancing. After a few days sleeping next to the big lake, I usually feel like I've been filled up with nourishment and topped off with vitality and peace. Conditions can be bright, sunny, and calm enough to see down into the cool blue depths as the water tempts the hardiest of us to wade until our legs go numb; or, as is usually the case, it can be damp, foggy, and chilly enough for wool sweaters as waves crash against the rocky shore. She's a lake of many moods, but regardless of where her mood falls on a particular day or season, she's a healer as much as she's an enchantress.

A few weeks ago, my family celebrated my parents' 40th wedding anniversary along the shore near the little hamlet of

Grand Marais. We rented a house-turned-cabin at an old resort, hiked through the cold mist for the first four days and emerged into bright sunshine toward the end of our stay. We skirted the sides of ancient mountains, traversed bridges made from logs and stuck our feet into the cool water of inland lakes that you can only get to by hiking trail. We watched loons dive, sat in front of a massive stone fireplace, and gazed out at a horizon that seems to disappear into forever. We poked around on the rocky shore, explored the inland tide pools and marveled at all the shades of green that moss can be. We remembered that we are part of the lake just as much as she is part of us and the rest of the earth.

We remember that though we need to visit her regularly, we also need to remember how it feels to be along her rocky shores when we aren't physically there. We need to remember to tap into that feeling when we are unbalanced or adrift, no matter where on the earth we find ourselves. Because her energy is made of ours, and ours is made of hers. And we are all made of the same stuff as stars.

A Name

A thing is right when it tends to preserve the
integrity, stability and beauty of the biotic community.
It is wrong when it tends otherwise.
–ALDO LEOPOLD

Fireweed Farm. That's my favorite option for a name for the
garden that we are aiming to get off the ground in the next few
years. Too bad it's taken already by a lovely farm in Palmer,
Alaska. That's ok. I haven't actually seen any fireweed on the
land, so it probably wasn't a good choice. But I liked it because
fireweed is the first plant to come back after a forest fire, so it
symbolizes new life, fresh beginnings and bringing something
good out of something that is broken—all things that are consistently part of a farm or garden. There are new things going
on all the time, and each growing season is its own unique web
of life. Parts of the web end each fall with the first hard frost
but there is always the promise of another spring just over the
horizon. That, and it just sounds neat.

Right now it feels like we bypassed the last of spring and
went directly to August or Arizona, as it is currently 101 degrees outside. We have little fledgling plants out in the raised
beds and new berries, potatoes, broccoli and onions up in the

big field, so with any luck they will weather the heat and breezy conditions without too much complaint (aka withering). The newest section of the field has been tilled under and black plastic mulch has been laid on part of it eagerly waiting to house the flats of plants that are sitting on the front lawn in their 4 inch pots. They will get planted. We will water, mulch, compost and weed. Plants will grow. Some plants will not or will get eaten by the resident deer or raccoons. Maybe we'll get chickens. Neighbors will be curious and conversations will begin. Relationships will build. We will spend time outside no matter what the weather forecasters say. We will harvest and we will preserve. Soil will improve and a new farm organism will start to grow. We will nurture a sustainable way of living. We will practice what we preach. And start to preach what we practice. We will continue, even if we don't do it right some of the time.

We might not be Fireweed Farm, but we are something. Something that needs a name that can live up to what we want to be. American Indians—many of the tribes that lived in the area where we now are—have a tradition of being given spirit names after they start to get older—a spirit name, or the "Indian name" tells something about the individual, such as a piece of their personality, their mission in life, or their gifts to the community. In some indigenous cultures, a name is selected when a commitment is made to a spiritual life. How do we name a lifestyle, a commitment to a way of being, an evolving of habitat, a community centered in sharing and a common respect? Good question. We'll think of a name at some point—it won't be perfect but nothing is, so we'll be content with whatever the outcome. In the meantime, let the growing continue.

Part Two

Summer

Then followed that beautiful season... Summer....
Filled was the air with a dreamy
and magical light; and the landscape
Lay as if new created in all the freshness of childhood.
—Henry Wadsworth Longfellow

Ah, summer. The time of the year when the days are long and life seems to somehow speed up and slow down at the same time. The work around the land and garden is demanding, but the days are long and support our efforts with the grace of lingering light and warmth. There is time to play and rest amidst the needs of caring for the garden and household. The cool rush of water over bare skin in the evening, the feel of the warm wind whistling the scent of hot pine down into the valley, the way a tomato tastes like a burst of sunlight straight off the vine...these details bring out the color of the days and remind me that the earth does indeed laugh in flowers, as Emerson wrote all those years ago. Summer is paddling and running through forests, sleeping outside and slapping at mosquitoes. It is finding ticks and going back outside anyway. It is the neighborhood buzzing with activity because everyone is outside more than any other time of the year. It is feeling bone weary at the end of a long hot day in the sun and collapsing in gratitude for the opportunity to be alive. It is thunderstorms and picnics, nurturing and sowing, and giving and taking in the dance of abundance.

Cultivating Community

Earlier in the year, I read an article in *Taproot Magazine* about something called the Portland Preservation Society. The goal of the society is to provide a forum for swapping homemade food—in their case, mostly canned goods. They meet monthly; usually in people's homes, in each other's gardens, and even sometimes at local businesses to talk food, food preservation, support each other's efforts in living sustainably and go home with a variety of things that they probably wouldn't have made themselves.

It made me want to move to Portland and join.

And since I actually like Minnesota winters and have a community and little piece of land that I am extremely grateful to call home, it seemed like the next best thing to moving across the country to swap homemade food was to start a local group.

Enter the St. Croix Valley Food Swap.

The plan was to gather a loose collective of St. Croix Valley (eastern Minnesota and western Wisconsin along the St. Croix River area) food/sustainable living enthusiasts to meet monthly to swap homemade goods—though participation is certainly open to anyone who wants to join, regardless of geographical area. (So, if you live in Portland and want to travel to Minnesota to swap, you are most welcome.)

Like the Portland group, when I pitched the idea to some neighbors, I saw no need for bartering or bidding on items, nor for a cover charge to attend. They've encouraged participants to bring up to five items to share at each meeting: a good model to follow. Some examples of what people might bring to trade are: jams, jellies, marmalades, chutneys, relishes, pickles, pestos, spreads, sauces, extracts, beverages, infused alcohols, any variety of preserved fruits and vegetables, flavored salts, granolas, breads, eggs, goat soaps, hand knit washcloths, and more. Seasonal fresh produce from your garden? Fabulous. A great soup you made too much of? Awesome. Beeswax candles? Certainly. Honey from your hives? Wonderful. Pre-packaged treats from the grocery deli? Not so much.

The goal here is to promote and share the energy that builds from making things ourselves from the abundance that can be found in the local community and from sharing the fruits of our labors with each other. At the meetings, participants choose one item at a time to take home until all the items are distributed, and each participant gets as many items as he or she brought to share. Good conversations are had, ideas are shared, knowledge grows and new friendships come into being. Community is cultivated, and our dependence shifts another inch toward our neighbors instead of what we can buy at the local big box store.

Sounds pretty good, right? I thought so. I hope it works. The first swap in June was a success, and I took home canned peaches, chai tea, fresh eggs and spaghetti sauce. Frances Moore Lappe writes, "Every aspect of our lives is, in a sense, a vote for the kind of world we want to live in." I want to live in a world that includes sharing and is comprised of communities that take care of each other and the earth. A tall order perhaps, in this day and age, but tall orders need to be fulfilled, too. I'm not changing mine any time soon.

Practicing Resurrection

June always holds a sense of emptiness for me—not in a negative way, just in a way that reminds me that for a really long time, "working at camp" and everything that comes along with what that means defined my summers. From 1998 to 2004, Lutheran Outdoor Ministry was a huge piece of the filter through which I viewed the world, and it still colors how I choose to observe what goes on around me. The scent of pine needles on a hot day in August will probably always transport me instantly to a shared footpath in an alpine forest, or a lodge deck peppered with distant laughter in a misty valley, or the sunny banks of a scenic river way.

At Lee Valley Ranch in Custer, South Dakota, I lived in a tent and spent the months just out of high school as a Ranch Hand. It meant leading games for children who attended retreats, washing a lot of dishes, learning the rules of Cricket from the Australians on staff and falling for the long-haired guitar player/campfire song leader/guy who every 18-year-old female had a crush on that summer. I learned to lead day hikes and pack a backpack and play three chords on the guitar. I felt like I was an essential part of helping the place function. I felt like I mattered, and I felt like I belonged there.

At Luther Heights, outside of Ketchum, Idaho, I lived in a storage shed turned bunk house and spent two summers as an Assistant Cook. It meant learning how to bake seven loaves of bread at one time, jumping in the icy waters of Lake Alturas on beach day, figuring how to pack the right amount of trail food for backpacking groups, and getting dolled up on weekends to go into town. It meant living in the shadow of two mountain ranges and waking up to the smell of pine needles and wearing Teva sandals. It meant relaxing in the director's wood fired hot tub on working weekends. I got into and out of my first long distance relationship and made hundreds of friendship bracelets. I felt like I was an essential part of helping the place function, and I was, for those summers. Everyone there was. I felt like I mattered, and I felt like I belonged there.

At Luther Park, in Danbury, Wisconsin, I split time between a cabin on stilts and a tent on the banks of the Namekagon River. My last two summers in college were spent as a Canoe Guide/Outpost Counselor. It meant shepherding groups of teenagers down the river in canoes for a week at a time, starting a lot of campfires, swimming across Lake 26 with a lifeguarding tube and making sure the Whisper Light camp stove didn't explode when it got a fuel leak. It meant checking for ticks on a regular basis, making friends with the 'rough around the edges' camp cook and spending the weekends on the shores of Lake Superior. I met another guitar player and fell in love and turned 21. I felt like I was an essential part of making the place function, and the place turned into an essential piece of what made me function. I felt like I mattered, and I felt like I belonged there.

At Sky Ranch, on the northern border of Rocky Mountain National Park, I lived in the nature center where my Dad lived 30 years before as a backpacking guide. That summer I was the camp Naturalist. It meant quitting the first "real" job that I got after graduating college, spending the summer away from my future spouse and finding my own way of being in the midst of strangers who turned into lifelong friends. It meant being the lead guitarist at campfires because the only other people with any guitar playing skills were backpacking guides who were always out on the trail. It meant weekends at a riverside hippie bar and skinny dipping in icy alpine lakes. It meant hiking and running and being a part of a place that was a part of me before I was born. I felt like I was an essential part of making the place function, and the place reminded me of my roots and my strength. I felt like I mattered, and I felt like I belonged there.

And then, after quitting my second "real" job, I found myself back at Luther Park again. I lived in the Log House and spent my last camp summer as the Waterfront Director. It meant afternoons spent counting campers in the water to make sure they were all safely accounted for and driving a fully loaded 15 passenger van while pulling a canoe trailer. It meant facilitating waterfront emergency drills and watching the staff dive into the ice-cold early summer water on my count. It meant feeling a little adrift as one of the "old" staff members. It meant letting my future spouse reclaim the role of lead guitarist, wondering what I was going to do after another summer ended, and trying to hold onto the strength I had uncovered over the years. It meant being in a place as an essential part of the whole, and it meant holding that wholeness as my foundation even on the days that were punctuated by more struggle and uncertainty that I was prepared for. Even in the midst of challenge, I felt like I mattered, and I felt like I belonged there.

There are many who say that organized religion is on its way out, that the church is dying, and that no one wants to commit to being a part of something that feels like a sinking ship. Maybe it's true. Maybe the hole in the stern it too big to patch. But I think that perhaps even as 'church' fades, or evolves, the thing that will remain steadfast is what was most important in the first place. Church at its core is community. It's an energy that is bigger than anything humanity alone can imagine. It's being taken care of, and it's taking care of others. People want to feel like they are an essential part of something. That they matter. That they belong. They want to see life unfolding and they want to be part of the new growth. Like a camp, church is a place—but it's a place that has to be found outside of, despite, or perhaps even in the midst of a burning building's walls.

It's been well over 10 years since I was on staff at wilderness-based outdoor youth camp, leading games and day hikes and prayers. These days I wouldn't last more than a half a week in a cabin full of 12 year olds with only an hour off per day. But what sticks with me, and always will, is the feeling of being part of something that is hard to put into words. It's that feeling of being essential, of deep belonging and of community without borders that shines a light into places that might have otherwise remained unexplored. It's the feeling of peace that can stay present despite the "emptiness" that can be left behind after a fire goes through. The emptiness, the new space that was made visible only by something old passing away, shows us to a gate that leads into a world that lies beyond what we can clearly see right now. As Jim Hubbell writes, "Our task is to walk through and discover where the gate leads."

Maybe the emptiness that I sense in June each year is simply a reminder of the newness that can come from the passing of the old into the life that waits beyond. To use the words of Wendell Berry, perhaps we could all benefit from remembering to *practice resurrection*.

A Cry for
Our Common Home

Summer Solstice in the northern hemisphere: The cusp of summer. The frogs are singing their songs down by the lake, the garden is growing almost as fast as the weeds, and my daughter is snuggled up in her bed as dusk falls on this, the longest day of the year. The earth continues to move through her cycles, and she does so right alongside the actions of humanity that take place on her crust. Though her crust is peppered with blemishes, hardship and the ruts of transition, spring is still turning to summer, at least this year.

And a few days ago, Pope Francis released an encyclical on climate change, the environment and inequality. You've probably seen talk of it if you've spent any time looking at the news or online in the last few days. It's the first one to include these topics, and that alone makes it something to notice and at least skim. I haven't read the whole thing, and I probably won't. But a few excerpts did stand out, one being the following, "These days, they [the global poor most affected by climate change] are mentioned in international political and economic discussions, but one often has the impression that their problems are brought up as an afterthought, a question which gets added almost out of duty or in a tangential way, if not treated merely as collateral damage. Indeed, when all is said and done, they frequently remain at the bottom of the pile. This is due partly to the fact that many professionals, opinion makers, communications media and centres of power, being located in affluent urban areas, are far removed from the poor, with little direct contact with their problems. They live and reason from the comfortable position of a high level of development and a quality of life well beyond the reach of the majority of the world's population. This lack of physical contact and encounter, encouraged at times by the disintegration of our cities, can lead to a numbing of conscience and to tendentious analyses which neglect parts of reality. We...must integrate questions of justice in debates on the environment, so as to hear both the cry of the Earth and the cry of the poor."

At risk of making sweeping generalizations, Pope Francis hits on an essential element in the discord we are experiencing in this modern world, the one he says is starting to "look like an immense pile of filth." He calls out our world leaders for being separate. From the poor, as you read above. But I also read that to mean that our world leaders, like so many of us, are cut off from the Earth itself.

It's challenging to look past the market trends and economic disasters into the real issues (deforestation, species extinction, water degradation, habitat loss, etc..) when one spends the majority of one's time looking at screens, worrying about how to pay off debts to another world powerhouse or in meetings where the illustrations are charts, graphs and numbers. When priorities are centered around growing the economy, making more money and creating jobs to make more stuff to make more money, the natural world suffers. People suffer. Animals and plants suffer. Even those policy makers and the so called

"1%" suffer. When we as a people live cut off from nature, life in all forms suffers.

We haven't reached the point where the majority of people accept that our systems need to change. There have been plenty of natural disasters, economic crashes, and unacceptable behavior among our species to illustrate that things are simply not working. There are entire island nations being swallowed by the sea, leaving thousands of creatures, including humans, searching for new lands to call home. The evidence is glaringly transparent if we choose to see it. What's not in place yet is the acceptance that things are where they are, and that in order for humanity to thrive in harmony with the Earth and the rest of creation, we need to let go of our cycle of "more, better, faster" and accept "enough" in its place. We might find that "enough" ends up providing more abundance than we thought possible.

I like to think that Pope Francis's public statement is a sign that despite myriad differences in beliefs and value systems, people have the capacity to acknowledge that the one constant across the board is the Earth. Her health is our health. Her life is our life. As Wendell Berry writes, "The earth is what we all have in common."

Can we be the change, as Gandhi once said? I hope we can. It won't be easy. Change, even if we shut down the energy grid right now, is going to be slow. It won't happen overnight, even though we want it to. Those island nations will probably be just a memory in 50 years, and we need to feel the grief of what has already come to pass. Change will take planning and doing things that make us feel uncomfortable and stretch our boundaries. We will have to talk to people we don't like. As Pope Francis writes, "We need a conversation which includes everyone, since the environmental challenge we are undergoing, and its human roots, concern and affect us all."

North House

I can drive north on Interstate 35, and after a few hours, I hit Duluth—an inland harbor city on the shores of America's largest freshwater lake. Lake Superior greets me with a blast of cooler air, a view of the lift bridge, and some fog as I crest a large hill and start the descent to lake level. A twisty route through the maze of ramps and tunnels that punctuate the city center eventually invites me to merge onto MN Hwy 61. I take the right turn, drive past some of Duluth's oldest and grandest lakeside manors and exit the city, still heading north and now slightly east. With the lake to my right and a thick forest to my left, I continue on my way, noticing the purple lupines in the ditches and tiny rain-fed waterfalls in all of the rocky formations that are exposed due to continued updates to the road as the years progress. As I continue northeast past the little town of Two Harbors and leave the last fast food chain joint behind, I can feel time slow down. I still have 50+ miles to go to my destination, but somehow I feel like the rush to get there is over. The pace of life is slower here, far from the city and away from things like multiple lane freeways and shopping malls.

And eventually I do get to my destination, after a few short excursions down footpaths into the dense forests of the state parks along the route or out onto rocky outcroppings that allow a gaze of moody water that seems to go on forever. Grand Marais, another harbor town of much smaller scale than Duluth, invites me in as I drive up a gentle slope, past a canoe outfitter, the local radio station and a campground. The road looks like it will take the car straight into the big lake, and I welcome the sensation of immersing myself in the energy of the place.

The North House Folk School—a pocket of brightly colored, large timbered buildings, wood fire smoke and wooden boats—holds some of that energy. When I walk onto the small campus, I hear the sounds of hammers, conversation and the clanking of boat moorings. I smell bread baking in a wood fired masonry oven and notice the scent of the neighboring fisherman's catch being prepared for lunch. I take a seat on a bench made from an old timber beam, its surface worn smooth from all the bodies it has supported over the 18 years that this place has been in operation. Gazing out at the harbor, past the breakwater, I see the Hjordis, the school's 50 foot schooner, coming in from an afternoon excursion on the lake, its maroon sails demonstrating why it has become icon of the harbor.

This is a place where things are done slowly, with intention. Traditional crafts are taught and learned with a sense of reverence—of wonder—that an act as simple as carving a spoon from a piece of wood can be so powerful to the soul. It is a place that is dedicated to the act of creating something that is going to last—something that is unique and real because it was made by hands that were eager to embrace the creating as much as the outcome. There is a sense of being able to grab onto the energy of this place and make it into whatever you need it to be. Things are possible, here. This is a place that will show you what it means to interact with your environment in a way that will sustain you for years to come. This is a place that honors the past and the future in the same breath.

I meander around campus for a while, have dinner at the Angry Trout Café next door and head back south on the road to my campsite. A gentle rain is falling, but the tangible energy remains unshakable despite the fog that hangs over the landscape. When it is time to go home, I wonder if I'll be able to remember to honor the breath of the handmade and sustainable as the days click by, virtual remains part of life and quickness threatens to dictate. I wonder if this place will be able to hold space for stillness and intention and craft even if the roadway continues to get wider. I wonder what it is about this energy that speaks to a woman wearing deer skins, a man sporting high-tech hiking clothes, and a biker decked out in full leathers via a language they can all understand. I wonder what it is about this place that makes people curious and open to other perspectives.

But at the end of the day, I realize I know. Perhaps all people crave stillness and a sustainable pace at their core no matter what they do with the surface of their lives. And perhaps the act of making something tangible with our own two hands, or being around the energy that is produced by such an act, is one way to remember and honor that craving.

I can drive north and back again, and I can take the energy of a place that celebrates cultivating traditional ways of life and let it seep deep into my bones and then out into the world one intention, acted on, at a time.

Light Through Lettuce

I dropped off a food shelf donation this morning. Lettuce, kale and cucumbers are starting to show signs of being abundant out in the garden, so it felt like time to share. I rolled into the Family Pathways dusty parking lot, walked into the pole building-turned-donation center and handed a bag of fresh, organic produce to the volunteer who was working. Onto the scale it went and came in at a whopping two pounds. Lettuce doesn't weigh much. And greens and cucumbers don't provide much bulk for someone who is trying to make each calorie count. Earlier in the morning, I had hesitated to even bother donating something that seemed so insignificant. But the hope that lettuce that has enjoyed a cool, wet spring in our garden will find its way into a meal for someone who might not otherwise have gotten something fresh and healthy won out.

The volunteer wrote up a receipt, said a heartfelt thank you, and I promised to bring more when it becomes available. The entire exchange took approximately six minutes. I got back in the Jeep, rolled down the window to let in the morning air and was on my way to the next thing.

So, even though those six minutes seemed like just a blip on the screen of a day, I can remember that even though some lettuce and cucumbers and kale might not fill a hungry belly that wants more protein, the love and commitment to a healthy community and earth will somehow fill in some of the gaps. They may lack caloric bulk but the energy that those vegetables carry with them has the potential to shine a small bit of light, wherever they end up.

It turns out no act of giving is insignificant. Every gift has value, and every act of kindness has the ability to shine light where it is needed. Even lettuce.

Contact

This morning I really wanted to stay in bed. The room was dark, the sheets were cool, and my husband was still sleeping soundly. I wanted to lay there, and then get up at my leisure, check my email and drink coffee. So instead of letting myself lay there and think about getting up and what I really wanted to do, I just got up. Somehow I managed to turn off my thinking and stumble through the physical motions of putting feet on the floor, gathering up clothes, getting a drink of water and finding the keys. I got in the Jeep, drove 5 miles southeast and crossed the St. Croix River into the little town of Osceola, Wisconsin. It's situated high on the bluffs overlooking the river valley, and the river this morning was as smooth as glass. I didn't stop at the river today though, I continued on and went north through the downtown area as shops set up for the day and open signs flickered on. At County Road S, I turned left and found myself at the little parking area for one of Wisconsin's "State Natural Areas."

There are 373,000 acres spread out between 673 natural areas across the state, and they are used for research and education, the preservation of genetic and biological diversity and for providing benchmarks for determining the impact of use on managed lands. I appreciate them because they tend to be punctuated with more wildness and unknowns and refreshing energy than the surrounding more peopled areas. At any rate, this one on County S has proven to be a place where I can recalibrate or refocus when needed. Apparently this morning my body needed recalibration, and that need won out over my mind telling me to just do the same old routine.

I parked the Jeep in the empty lot and tied my keys into the laces of the ugliest pair of trail running shoes I've ever had and started jogging into the tree cover. (Why are all women's trail running shoes pink, or purple or turquoise or some other neon color?) The trail starts wide and takes you down to the river backwaters if you go straight. Today I turned left to cross the wooden footbridge over a spring fed creek and started running down a single track through a stand of tall pines. This single track takes you deep into the woods, and it's always dark back there, no matter how bright the sun is shining. And quiet. It's like someone turned the volume down and bumped up the contrast—it's easier to notice the details, even when running. There are always deer and squirrels and a myriad of other small creatures scurrying about on the forest floor. One spring I almost stepped on a tiny spotted fawn, likely just days old, lying in the middle of the trail.

Today I followed the loop trail quickly and had two white-tail deer for company while deep in the woods, a Pine Marten looking me in the eyes from a dead tree that had fallen across the path at the midpoint, and the sound of rushing waters moving downward toward the river valley after turning to follow the ridge of the creek bed back to the footbridge. I was reminded why it's important to have contact with wild things. It brings things back into perspective and invites wonder into the ordinary, even if just for a moment.

Just 45 minutes after arriving, I was back at the parking area to head home into my work day. And now as I sit here looking at this screen, I'm glad I listened to the urge to recalibrate, and to make contact with the unpredictable nature of the things that inhabit the unpeopled places. Knowing that there are places with cold, tumbling water and deer grazing amidst a backdrop of the open space above the river valley and Pine Martens at home in trees that seem to reach up endlessly toward the sky...knowing these things exist in the world is enough to remind me what's real. It's not what's on the screen.

The Other Side of the Road

I've been a runner for many years, and consequently, I have logged a lot of miles on foot. I've run on pavement, dirt trails, golf courses, and beaches. I've run in past high rises, through suburbia, around cities and in the midst of cornfields and pine forests. Currently, I run a 2 mile loop around the tiny lake that backs up to the house almost every day. It's not far, and I don't usually go very fast during the heat of the summer, but this time outside, re-connecting to the energy of my immediate surroundings helps to keep me centered in reality. It keeps my physical body's cardiovascular system functioning in an efficient way, it gives my leg muscles some exercise and it forces me to pay attention to where I'm placing my feet.

I've had issues in the last few months with some mild discomfort in my right ankle that has worked its way up into the shin/calf area of my leg. It hasn't been enough to keep me from heading out each morning, but it has been enough for me to notice it and wish it didn't feel that way. It has been enough to invite a sense of dread when heading on a run when I'd rather be looking forward to enjoying the movement.

I got some new shoes, hoping that would help. It didn't. I wore my old shoes again. No change. I tried running with different posture and just got frustrated that I wasn't enjoying my running anymore due to trying to place my feet in a way that didn't seem natural. I started to feel like perhaps my body was just unbalanced and it was just something I was going to have to accommodate—or that I was simply going to have to stop running. And then a few days ago, as a last ditch effort, I ran on the other side of the road.

Most of my route is on gravel, on a road that slopes down just slightly on each side, presumably to allow proper drainage. Good for infrastructure and road maintenance, but not so good for human bodies when they always run on the same side. Due to always being just slightly tilted while in motion, my right ankle finally started to protest. And now, since I started running on the other side (yes, the "wrong" side, with traffic instead of against which is another matter entirely), the pain has minimized. I will, of course have to switch back and forth to avoid developing pain in the left side, stay mindful of my posture and pay attention to my foot placement in order to continue running successfully. But, at least for now, it's nice to know that the answer was less complicated than I anticipated.

There are a lot of issues that are not so easily solved: Humans as a whole continue to use more resources than the planet can sustainably provide, multitudes are exploited every day by the choices made by a wealthy minority, and the corporate culture of more, better, faster continues to pervade everyday life for far too many souls. But despite the dire state of so much of the world, it is heartening to know that sometimes the solution is as simple as running on the other side of the road. Perhaps some of our answers lie in looking for ways to do the things we do every day just differently enough to have an impact that contributes to healing instead of destruction.

Extinct Waterfalls

The other day I saw a hummingbird drink from a waterfall that dried up thousands of years ago. This tiny creature, glittering in the sunlight, lapped up a trickle of moisture that found its way to this remnant of before, situated high above a roadway and made into a spectacle for hikers to view from a platform.

I could imagine what the cliff used to look like, cascading water falling into a crystal clear pool at the base, flowing down into the great river deep in the valley. Water plants of all kinds probably covered the ground around the pool, and moss the hue of emeralds perhaps lined the cool back wall of the cliff, hidden by the falls. It was a pocket of myth and moisture—a sanctuary for all creatures who needed those things. The roadway site was likely just a swath of trees and more sandstone, maybe a route for elk or black bears on their way to drink from the river. Maybe there were people who walked there. Maybe they walked somewhere else. They walked more lightly than people do now, wherever their paths were. I could see them, too. They are us—our memories and our dreams.

All those years ago, when our memories were now and the forest was all there is, the waterfall was still a spectacle, but of a different kind. It wasn't something to hike to on a day off, a photo opportunity, or an excuse to stop to rest and check for cell service. Rather, it was an intricate part of the organic, living landscape. Not a separate point of interest, just an oasis amidst even more abundance, another piece of the paradise that lives again when we listen for it and help it to grow and harmonize with our own energy.

When hummingbirds drink from extinct waterfalls, memories bubble to the surface and transcend how we view time—despite the roadways and platforms.

We remember we are part of the ancient and still find our home in the present.

Finding Our Balance

There has been a lot going on lately. So many people I encounter say this, or allude to it, regardless of their life situation—poor, wealthy, middle class; student, teacher, parent; volunteer or employee; retiree or entry level worker. The pace of life is fast, quickening even as these words are typed. It's summer. The days are long. Opportunities to keep moving are everywhere. It would seem that all people are busy, constantly.

Yet steeped in the busyness, systems are changing, albeit slowly. A lot of energy is being projected into helping the population interact in a different, more positive and healthy way, and a project of that scale takes time and effort. Even those who do not recognize or believe that anything is different put a lot of time and effort into completing their usual tasks and going about their daily routines. Work hours are long, jobs feel tedious, values are tested, traffic is bad, cities are congested and the kids have music lessons, sports, day camp, tutoring sessions, and summer reading lists. All of which they need help with, or a ride to. The lawn has to be mowed and the dishes washed. Things take longer than anticipated and many times don't go quite as planned. So, regardless of state of being or level of awareness, people are generally busy and have too much to do.

How can we find a sense of balance amidst the energy that needs to be put out? How do we maintain our equilibrium when putting forth the energy that must back the tasks that need to be accomplished, the ideas that need to be thought of and implemented, and the hours of work that are necessary to move this planet into a way of existing that is sustainable and life giving for all? How can we take the ashes of failure and see an opportunity to know beauty in a completely different way?

For positive change to occur, we will all need to contribute and use our unique gifts to serve the collective. We will need to step outside of our individual needs and into our neighbors'. We will need to figure out how to operate cooperatively after so many years of competition. We will need to let go of needing more. Even the Joneses can't sustain their pace forever. We will need to accept sadness and allow joy to radiate from places of darkness. The road into the light, while welcoming and full of joy, is not without rocks, bumps and the occasional uphill stretch.

It sounds daunting, and maybe it is. But I think we can find our balance amidst the rocks, the uphill stretches and the energy needed to sustain momentum by remembering what is driving us to do the work in the first place. We can remember the vision of an earth that is defined by beauty, equality and peace. We can remember that this vision will not look the same to everyone, and that it doesn't have to. As we project the energy of love and joy into the space that surrounds every action and thought we will get where we are called to be, even if the road looks different than we thought it would. And we can use the empty space that exists around the work doing and being whatever it is that makes life real for us.

No one is asking for my advice, but here's some anyway: Take your life situation for what it is—a situation—instead of a sentence or definition; busy or not, and let it be a way for your Being, your true self, to experience all that is worth

A Forest's Peace

To walk into the forest is to walk in the space of possibility. As I walk, I look up and see the manifestations of another season reaching curled tendrils out into the world, inviting new growth and expansion. Looking horizontally offers a sense of existing in the right place, secure in my own space within the contrasts that define each breath I take. When I glance down, I feel deep into the earth and into the endless possibilities that lie under the surface, ready for the time when they are called to venture into being.

Walking through the dappled sunshine, I trail my hand over the bark of adolescent trees and the prickly remnants of last year's ferns, meandering toward somewhere else, undefined, yet magnetic in its pull. I don't quite know what brought me into this place where trees hold vigil and wildflowers pay homage to the peacekeepers, but I keep walking. Each step draws me further into the vastness that is found in each leaf, each blade of grass, each seed, each bit of soil. The air is cool here, with just a hint of moisture that invites a sense of ease and makes me feel tranquil in my body. I sense that it is important that I am right here, now. I sense that there is a possibility here that can be unfolded and put on like a new skin. I sense that I will not completely shed the old, but the new will enhance what already is and invite a fresh brightness when it is allowed to uncurl.

The forest is our teacher; our guide. It is ancient yet always new, wise and searching, strong but fragile. Through its evolution and growth we can see our own. The forest is a mirror of our past and a glimpse into our future. It is the present. It can show us the pain of the world, and it can provide a canvas for great beauty. The forest can show us healing, and it can teach us how to let joy rise from the depths of sorrow. It holds onto peace for us when we let it slip through our fingers, and when we can't see past our own searching. It forgives when we don't remember our own possibilities and when we tumble into the vastness that gives everything life with our eyes closed, instead of open.

I keep walking, making sure that my presence does nothing but add to the texture of creation's beauty as I drink in the clean air and exhale back into the flow of the forest's ancient rhythms. My mind is still foggy about what draws me onward, but the journey continues. A solitary leaf falls into my path, and as it settles onto the woodland floor I know that this path will continue.

Peace, unencumbered, walks here too, in the forest.

Crimson Flowers

You can walk up a short dirt trail that angles up from the house to the garden. Right now it is speckled with dry leaves, sticks and not enough moisture. At 7PM, the sun is just starting to sink below the aspen trees that watch over the western corner of the field, and tangerine shadows bounce between the blades of wispy grass and slide down into the valley. The ground is dry—it hasn't rained for weeks—but the plants are persistent and continue to grow and produce berries, tomatoes, squash and beans. Morning glories creep over the fence that surrounds the kale and chard patch, crimson flowers that blink open with the sunrise close again as evening blankets the landscape. The grass is tall and brown, and the weeds and wildflowers have much of the larger winter squash field in their clutches. Cool, misty air slides down into the valley when the conditions are right. The atmosphere holds a sense of calm despite the occasional car that speeds by on the dusty gravel road.

This patch of ground is somewhere in between the things that make up everyday life right now. We have a mortgage on the house, but this patch of land is ours, debt free. Farming is not our livelihood at the moment, but parts of this plot sustain us and provide food. Roads and moderate development frame two sides of this space, but the land itself is teeming with wild things in the form of big bluestem that sways with the slightest breeze, a gnarled old oak that keeps watch over the adolescent maple forest, and the fox that hunts voles in the snow come winter. There are new people in the community who value what we value and who want to talk about it. We are situated on the edge of something—the edge of moving into a different way of being, a different way of interacting with the everyday, a different path than what we may have been called to follow before. Today this spot on the earth is a part of that something. Maybe it won't always be. But today it is, and when the sun slides down past the aspen trees in the evening, casting shadows of hope and peace, something in the earth lights up and reminds us that being awake and staying that way can mean more than one thing—it's just up to us to continue to expand our awareness and walk into the present.

As the sun rises in the east at the birth of each dawn, spreading cleansing energies into the earth and her inhabitants, we are reminded to breathe in light and truth. Maybe this piece of land, this spot on the earth, represents that truth, despite shadows of despair or doubt that linger in our thoughts, in our physical selves, and in our relationships with each other and the natural world. What if we can let go of that which does not serve and practice wanting what already exists? What we need is already here—this calm energy lives in the body, in the mind, in the spirit, and in our place. The essence of truth surrounds us and wraps us up in its brilliance, if only we let it do so. It's time to live this truth. If the sun can keep rising in the midst of the predawn darkness and flowers keep opening their petals to the promise of a new day, we as one can do the same.

You can walk up a short dirt trail that angles up from the house to the garden. Crimson flowers wait there, hoping we continue to notice.

Wind in the Pines

There isn't much in the way of a welcome after you make the turn up a short gravel road after seeing the brown highway "Nature Park" sign—just a rough map, a wooden sign letting one know that this place is in fact "Wind in the Pines" park, a steel gate and some rules about not driving your four wheeler down the path. I made a point not to lock the keys in the Jeep and started off through the tall grass that was hiding the trail. After 50 yards, the path narrowed and split in three directions—each marked with a little hiker badge on a post. I opted to go straight, and this took me from an open meadow into a dim white pine forest. Though overcast and a little chilly for July, the forest drew me in, and I was enchanted by the abrupt transition from prairie grass to towering trees. The piney scent, one that always sends a little piece of me back to summers spent in the mountains, seemed to seep out of every surface as I moved deeper into the woodland. I was reminded how powerful being away from projects, computers and roads can be, even if just for an hour or two.

The towering pines did indeed seem to whisper as I made my way through this community of stately beings. There is something mystical about an old white pine—the way their branches grow without a pattern, the sheer, straight posture of their trunks, the way they act as the elders of the woods, watching over the rest of the forest. Walking through them and over their fallen needles brought a perspective that can only be felt in a natural setting. Here I was another organism, a part of an organic system that was yet to be tainted by the progress that we humans like to further with each passing day. Not that progress is bad—but it sometimes pulls our perspective away from what is already good about life and our environment.

I continued up onto a ridge and marveled at the landscape—was this really only 10 minutes from my house? Up on the steep slope, I could see down into a fern lined ravine on either side of the trail, and I could hear water running from a source unseen. This piece of land is actually a Minnesota "State Scientific and Natural Area," set aside for study and preservation due to its diversity. I kept going through the diversity as the path suddenly dropped deep into the depths of the forest. I ignored a private property sign and kept going a few more steps to an enchanting little creek. I was now standing next to the confluence of the ravines and at the trail's conclusion—complete with bubbling spring. The cold, clear water rose straight up from under the ground and joined the stream as it continued on its way to the larger St. Croix River. Hopping around on the rocks, back and forth over the glassy water, I took in the peaceful and alive feeling of this little sanctuary.

A short steep scramble out of the ravine, a meander back through the pines and prairie grass and I was back at the circle lot, ready to bring my re-grounded perspective back into the "real" world.

Bits of Astonishment

About a month ago, my family and I pulled into the driveway after a great five days up along the north shore of Minnesota, still reveling in the tonic that is Lake Superior, anticipating a low key few days of unpacking before returning to the usual work schedule. We ambled down the path from the garage, happy to be out of the car and walked into the house to a putrid smell and reports that the septic alarm had been going off for an indeterminate amount of time in our absence. Awesome. Turns out a little creature of some sort had chewed through the cord that powered the septic pump, shorting it out. Could have been much worse. All and all and easy fix for Nick, and we were back in business. But the smell . . . remained. For another day we pondered just what could be making the kitchen stink. Eventually we followed some clues and found a decomposing mouse behind the fridge. Again, awesome. But we got rid of it, gave the cats a pep talk and life carried on. A few days later I got a call that my credit card number had been stolen and there was someone in Texas trying to charge a trip to Thailand on my Visa. And the grass needed to be mowed and the garden weeded. As June ended, the water heater broke, one of our indoor cats got out and was lost for a day and a half, and my retreat co-leader broke her foot and couldn't come to the retreat we had been planning for several months. And then the road construction workers cut the phone lines that run to our house and we were down phone and internet for several days. Not a big deal, really, except when you work from home calling people and working on the internet. Just as we started to think, "what else could possibly go wrong?" we shared a tense evening with a very excited bat in the living room and admitted to ourselves that we can no longer stand the squealing noise the dryer makes and either need to get a new one or fully commit to line drying. Easy in the summer, not as easy when it's below freezing. And the garage needs a new roof.

It's been a rough few months.

If we expand the bubble outside of my own little personal dramas, that, let's be honest, aren't that dramatic or dire, we see plenty of stories of war, planetary destruction, persistent inequality, rampant violence of all sorts, and so on.

So why the sob story? Yes, it's been a rough few months, and yes, there are things about our world that make me ache with the injustice that gets played out every single day, but as I breathe into the situations that seem so dark and dismal, I keep finding little bits of goodness that make me gasp in astonishment. Many of my personal scenarios could have been much more dire, and I could sift through each one to find the lesson or the positive aspect of the situation. Lots of people are worse off than I am, and my life is a cake-walk compared to what millions of others experience on a daily basis. So, I'm not talking about finding the 'silver lining' of a given situation. What I mean is that interspersed between things breaking and not going how I want them to go, there have been plenty of little bits of astonishment showing up alongside the messes. Nature has a sneaky way of reminding me that wonder is alive and well in the world, even amidst heartache, turmoil, and suffering.

The retreat that I was so worried about having to cancel ended up being a weekend of inviting others to step into their gifts, of truth telling, of letting go and of embracing fluidity. I woke up on the last morning of the event and paddled through calm water under a gently waking sky and felt the muscles that had been stretched the day before in yoga class remind me of the strength of women, the importance of wildness and the power of storytelling.

Astonishment.

The pole beans that I planted in May started to climb their teepee a few weeks ago, and I went out this morning after lamenting the slowness of the internet and noticed that they are starting to blossom. Then I dug three colors of potatoes, picked some kale, and found a baseball bat sized zucchini and three perfectly ripe Sungold tomatoes which I ate directly off the vine, their sweetness exploding in my mouth like a brilliant sunset.

Astonishment.

After a sweltering jog around construction equipment this afternoon, Eva and I ran through the garden hose squealing, and then, dripping wet and covered with sticky grass, we picked blueberries with the meticulous care and wonder that young children so easily encourage.

Astonishment.

And as this summer day starts to fade away, the sliding door to the back deck is letting in a cool breeze, and I can hear birds and frogs singing their evening melodies as dusk falls on the lake and the alert stillness of darkness settles in for a nightcap. I remind myself that I am breathing and alive on an earth that is generous enough to grant me the ability to witness these things.

Astonishment.

The beauty of life takes my breath away sometimes, and I find myself wishing I could remember to be astonished more often. There will always be hardship and challenge and things that break. But there will also be ripe tomatoes, blueberry stained fingers, the feel of a child's hand in my own and the call of a loon through the darkness. No matter how hard things get, there will always be little bits of astonishment to fill in the gaps.

Two more unarmed black men were killed by police in the last week, and America is seemingly more divided than ever before. Fights start over hashtags, stories get warped, and moms who exercise their right to protest a broken system get arrested. Wars continue over issues that most people won't ever understand, including those fighting the battles. Refugees try to find a new land to call home while others try to decide which cruise to go on next. Fires burn in California while floods wash through towns in the Midwest. But in the midst of the chaos and [justified] rage and [never justified] violence, people of all colors still join hands and protestors from opposing sides sometimes cross highways to stand together and pray for peace. People speak truths and things get uncovered and we breathe through another day.

Astonishment. I see you, and I invite you to stay.

Waterways

Nick and I put in at Fall Lake just outside the little town of Ely in the late afternoon. The forecast posted at the ranger station had not looked promising, and clouds were looming, heavy with rain, when we loaded the canoe and pushed off the shore. A faint breath of mist surrounded us as we began to get into a rhythm of paddling, ready for days free of virtual tasks, car travel and commotion. We entered the Boundary Waters Canoe Area Wilderness shortly after setting out and soon arrived at our first portage. As we approached the sandy shoreline we were greeted by a group of men and their motorized canoe, filled to the brim with gear, rolling down the rocky path on a set of little rubber wheels. They were in a hurry. "Looks like storms are headed this way. Time to get back to reality." They motored off toward the landing that we had just left. We watched them go and turned back toward the portage. The sound of the falls that led into the next lake rushed around us as we loaded ourselves up for a 100 rod walk in the woods into the next lake.

We reached the portage trail's end and set out again, navigating through a narrow lake dotted with little treed islands, looking for a place to camp as evening fell over the landscape. The thunderheads that threatened earlier had lost some of their menace, but the dampness remained. After scrutinizing the map and peering at the shore, we spotted the site we sought through a watery field of wild rice. Nick set up the tent as drizzle began to fall, I found a perfect bear bag tree, and we ate a simple dinner of noodles before turning in for the night to the sound of howling wolves.

Like late summer storms, wolves are a mysterious and slightly unsettling part of a Boundary Waters experience. They are not a threat to humans (we are more a threat to them) and are rarely seen, but it is still a little unnerving to hear them howling after the sun goes down. It is quite easy to imagine an entire pack right outside your tent. The first night out in the wilderness sometimes includes a little tossing and turning—it can be challenging to get used to the quality of silence that comes with being surrounded by trees and water instead of front lawn shrubs and roads.

Alongside that silence, there is an energy that blankets wild places that isn't present in cities and towns. And safety takes on a different meaning when you are away from the usual routine of digital tasks, sitting in an office and sleeping in a bed. It is quite curious how easy it is to imagine all the things that could be out to get us in the woods when—truth be told—we are just as likely to run into adversity inside the confines of a city. But outside the human made realm, there is the undercurrent of the unknown, the unpredictable. It's untamed. Wild. Often in our culture, "wild" is of the same vein as dangerous. We are taught to avoid danger. But isn't it more dangerous to live a life devoid of interactions that remind us what truly living in communion with the earth feels like?

Morning came in a dewy haze, and we hashed out our options. Do we just head back since it is supposed to rain pretty much constantly? Or do we keep pressing on into whatever the wilderness might offer up next?

We opted to keep going. We had our rain suits, our common sense and a craving to shake our foundations in a way that going back could never offer. We packed up camp, ate a little trail mix, tossed everything in the canoe and pushed off through wisps of wild rice and lily pads. The morning that had greeted us with a damp embrace was swiftly clearing, and the dreary chill was soon replaced with warm sunlight and calm waters. You just never know what you are going to get when you choose to exist in the wild. But what you do know is that your foundation is somehow more solid after each shaky encounter and you have a clearer view of what reality can look like. As Thoreau writes in *The Maine Woods*: "Contact! Contact!"

It has to do with contact.

Hints of Moonlight

I met my neighbor the other evening for a spur of the moment drink at the local pub. We've developed a friendship in the last few years, both being transplants into an area that boasts plenty of third and fourth generation farm families. We share a commitment to sustainable living, and we have toddlers of the same age. From afar perhaps that is where our similarities stop. She is of African heritage. I am German/Scandinavian. She can talk to anyone, anywhere, about anything. I've been known to have trouble keeping a conversation going with my own spouse about things that really matter to me. Both of her parents have passed away. Mine are thriving and visit often. She has experienced life in several cultures, including life as a refugee. I did a semester abroad in college and all things considered, it was pretty tame. She's seen suffering and has known the kind of fear and heartache that I can't even begin to imagine.

We sat down at the bar and ordered drinks and fries. We chatted about the kids, the garden, the weather. She joked with the bartender, we laughed. She shared that she's been in a dark place, that things are overwhelming and that she isn't sure how to shake off the shroud. I listened. She spoke of loss, and feelings of failure and asked what my biggest fears are. I tried to answer and couldn't come up with much. She talked about the sensation of feeling trapped and about how the abundant choices that color life in America make it harder to live in gratitude. I listened. I agreed. I said I understood when I did understand. Sometimes I didn't. She told me pieces of her story that were buried deep, yet remained visible, like the dirt under an avid gardener's fingernails. I didn't get all the details. I said "it's ok" when her eyes threatened to spill over. She apologized. I said I thought it was okay to feel whatever she needed to feel. She asked if I really meant it when I invited her to share what she needed to share. I said yes. I meant it. She wondered how to figure out who she really is. I said, "I wonder that, too."

At the end of the night I drove her back to her house, and she picked her way across a moonlit yard strewn with parts of remodeling projects and plastic toys. All of the questions remained. We hadn't come to any huge revelations or profound solutions to fix what feels wrong. We hadn't accomplished anything concrete, and she was still feeling adrift. Darkness has a way of lingering despite our best efforts to push it away.

As she was getting out of the car she thanked me for being there. For listening. Driving home down the gravel road we share, I wondered if it was enough.

I looked up as I got out of the car and was reminded that light has a way of showing up when darkness lingers too long, even if it's just a hint of moonlight in an ink black sky rolling with cloud cover. Maybe a few hours on bar stools is enough to invite light to take a seat close enough to soften some of the inky black into shadow.

Kayak Morning

To be alive is to totally and openly participate
in the simplicity and elegance of here and now.
–Donald Altman

I glide through the silence of early morning fog rising from the
river, my kayak paddle slicing through the glassy water, propelling me forward into the next moment, and the next, and the
next. I am not always good about doing this, but sometimes in
the time just after dawn as the sun starts to claim ownership
of the sky, I am able to be in each moment, not thinking about
the last one, not anticipating the next one. I'm just present, one
paddle slice or step or breath at a time. Simple elegance, on
paddle slice at a time.

We spent this past week about 500 miles from home, in a
little yellow cottage outside of Manistique, Michigan. Perched
on the southern shore of the state's upper peninsula and the
northern shore of Lake Michigan, my husband's family has
roots deep in the sandy shores and waters and lore of the small
lakeside town and its surrounding forests. It's a place of simplicity if you choose it, and an elegance of a different sort than
is usually conjured from the term. I suppose you could say it's
a place where they have always gone to be present. To simplify
the pace of the days and let the slow energy of a summer vacation take the reins.

My days during the week started with running down to Indian lake, the shallow, crystal clear source of the Manistique River that meanders at a leisurely pace for a few miles before flowing into Lake Michigan. After running through the tranquil energy of the quiet summer neighborhoods as the earth shook the sleep from her eyes, I donned a bathing suit and jumped in the river or into a kayak to baptize myself into a new day.

Every morning was ripe with the type of silence that can only be found in the hour just after dawn. I met two foxes playing chase in the dark woods down the road, paddled alongside countless ducks, heard the ancient call of the Sandhill crane and stared into the eyes of a deer who looked up from taking a drink. I saw moss and sand and huge white pines and tiny scrub brush co-existing peacefully and finding harmony with each other's differences. I felt the pulse of the wildness that still runs deep through that land, and it reminded me that there is indeed a simple elegance just waiting to be noticed around most every bend.

Everyone else was usually awake and moving by the time I was done with my little morning routine, and the day's pace picked up a bit as we went off to see the sights, but those mornings kept me grounded and conscious of the fact that simplicity and elegance are a choice, and a choice that I need to remember I have every single day. Even when vacation is over and the ordinary events of the days start to melt into each other. Even then.

It's good inspiration to try to keep getting up early to run in the heat of the summer. And paddle before work to get myself as close to the water as possible without dunking myself into the weedy depths of our little backyard lake. Note to self: Acquire kayak or way to transport small canoe down to the dock.

Contrast

It's August. Days range from cool and pleasant to hot and sticky. The ground is dusty because it hasn't rained in six weeks, but the forest floor still holds on to the last drops of moisture from a wet spring. The reeds by the lake are the tallest they've been in recent memory, and the lilac bushes are droopy and covered with a fine film of grit. The corn is tall and sends its scent out over the fields when the wind blows, and the potato plants are withering and giving their glory to the gems that lay below the surface. The August full moon is bright enough to squint at against the black night sky and makes the stars seem dim.

Many people are waiting. Others are living fully in the present, regardless of what it looks like right now. There are places that know great peace, and places that know too much about how sorrow and war can mold a life. There are people in the midst of war who know how to cultivate peace within themselves and hold that space for those who have not yet learned how. There are people residing in the midst of peaceful places who know nothing but sorrow and long to find what so many others around them have. Contrast can be seen everywhere, sometimes even within the same being.

What would our world be like without the contrast that it embodies today? Would beauty be less vibrant? Would the light look less bright without all the dark shadows that linger?

Would we be astonished at new beauty, unlike what has been before? Would we need new words to describe what is before us? We can only guess at what we might see when we let peace overshadow war, and when we no longer have to hold space for those who cannot find the truth in the present.

We might see days that are cool and pleasant, and days that are hot and sticky. We might walk over dusty ground and hope for rain and linger in a damp forest after a soggy spring. The reeds might be taller than ever and the lilacs might droop, covered in grit and the scent of corn might cascade over the fields with the wind. The August moon might be bright enough to cast shadows into the black sky of night. Maybe contrast will be still seen everywhere, but it will be found in the way you and I look at the stars differently, but with the same eyes.

It's August, and the moon is full. If we squint, we can see through the contrast and into the stars that still seem dim.

Hope Went Searching

It's been a long time since I've written about our organic farming aspirations. The garden is still out there, growing on the hillside and down in the valley in the field that became part of our homestead a few years ago. The sun still fades into night with the passing of the days, and the lake still shimmers in the moonlight. Back then, I had a lot of hope for what this garden might become, a lot of expectations about what life was going to look like, and a lot of excitement for what was happening. A lot has changed in the time that has passed since we acquired the land where we thought a market garden/CSA/biodynamic farm might operate someday. Our partners in the purchase of this farm-land have gone their separate ways, and for a while my hopes for the garden and living in a new way went with them. Some of my hope went west to begin again in the foothills of the Rockies, and some of my hope went even further, across the deep waters of the Pacific to try to find peace on an island. And some of my hope stayed on a small patch of land in Minnesota, waiting.

It's been almost two years since part of my hope went searching. I might never know for sure if it found what it needed so far from this little patch of land, but I don't think it matters if I find out. What does matter is that the hope that stayed is done waiting. The garden is still growing on the hillside and down in the valley, and though it might not be as large or productive or cooperative as I thought it might be by now, it's still there. There are tomato plants as large as small trees threatening to topple their stakes and more leeks than we will know what to do with when it's time to harvest them. There are potato plants full of blossoms and promise, an emerald green forest of kale, and trailing vines of squash, melons and cucumbers spreading their abundance over the ground. Squatty pepper plants and resilient berry bushes remain insistent on thriving despite their rough start. There is an apple tree and a cherry bush and a row of asparagus that will always hold a piece of the past, and of some of my hope that went searching. I want them to hold onto it.

Because this little patch of roots and stems and leaves and fruits and dreams is still fueling my hope for what is to come. New relationships were able to form that would not have formed otherwise, and souls got what they needed to evolve and maybe even start to heal. The direction the last two years decided to take allowed new space to uncurl in the midst of unexpected change. Because some of my hope went searching, and instead of getting lost in the wilds of the world, it grew and turned into peace.

I still have a lot of hope for what this garden, this patch of the earth, might become or represent. I also have a lot of hope for the peace that already is, has been and always will be regardless of whatever the winds of change bring next.

Full Circle

Today started brightly as the mid-summer sun cast its morning shadows over the gravel road that circles the lake, and the garden—perched on its hillside—gathered nourishment for another day of growing. After the recent rains, the dust has settled, and the earth feels cleaner and more vibrant than a week ago. To celebrate, and to start the day with something that felt tangible before firing up the work computer, I decided it was time to start pulling the beets out of the ground. After almost six weeks of dry weather, the rain that finally decided to return to our home soil made pulling the beets a much easier task than it would have been a few days ago. The last few growing seasons have been punctuated by too much moisture in the early months followed by Minnesota's version of drought as the faucet shuts off after mid-July. This year has been true to form—but two days ago we finally got some rain and the earth is rejoicing. For right now, anyway, the recent allotment of moisture has been just enough to perk things up and clear the air. At any rate, due to the ease of harvest I pulled enough beets to make a trip to the food shelf to share the bounty.

Eva and I pulled up to the pole building and brought our canvas bags full of produce into the storage room where we were greeted by the volunteers and staff.

"Wow, those beets look great. Thanks so much for bringing them in. Do you want some cabbage and green peppers?"

Wait. What?

It turned out Family Pathways had received a huge load of cabbage (as in thousands of pounds) and several pallets of peppers just hours before from another, much larger, food distribution organization. They didn't think they'd be able to find homes for all of the cabbages and peppers before they started to rot, so they were offering them to everyone who came through the doors.

We went in bearing beets and left with cabbage and peppers. We accepted someone else's too much as we gave our own and became part of the circle of enough.

Preservation

Trays of yellow, red, orange, green and pink tomatoes shine under the morning sun. Bell peppers of the same colors are piled high and purple eggplants and beets peek out from around wooden boxes of long, slender green and purple beans. Carrots the color of a sunset fill more trays. Leafy bunches of basil, oregano, thyme and parsley provide an aroma to inspire any aspiring chef. The display table of a farmer's market vendor in early September is much like a work of art—and it is a sight that tells a story of hard work, dedication to a piece of land and the love of a simple and sustainable lifestyle. And it provides plenty of ingredients for a weekend of putting up the harvest.

There is something undeniably real about taking plants that were grown from local soil, chopping them up, mixing them together, cooking them down and putting them into jars to be enjoyed in the depths of winter. In an era where one can get any type of food at any time during the year, there is something more real about not indulging in the "get it now" attitude and the unsustainable way of living that punctuates so much of the "developed" world. What if growing (or knowing the grower) and preserving food ourselves was our default, much going to the grocery store or Target tends to be? What if shopping meant waking up early to get first pick of the produce on Saturday morning? What if food meant gardens, pastures, and a freezer full of frozen fruit, veggies and sustainably raised meat? What if convenience food meant popping open a jar that spent time in a pressure cooker or snacking on fruit that once lined trays of a food dehydrator?

This past weekend was our annual food preservation family gathering—the goal each year is to preserve most of the fruits and vegetables we will need to get us through the winter and early spring before things start growing again in the Midwest. This year we succeeded in canning jar after jar of beets, salsa, tomatoes, and applesauce; we froze peppers, basil pesto, raspberry and plum jam and zucchini bread; we dehydrated eggplant, more tomatoes, peaches, hot peppers and herbs. The work was simple—harvest, chop, mix, jar and boil, freeze or dry. But through this simple work, a rhythm that is missing from a world of offices, supermarkets and interstates is always rediscovered. A sense of belonging to the earth, gratitude for what the earth can provide and appreciation for the hands that cultivate it is rekindled. As the shelves fill with jars, relationships deepen, feelings of accomplishment settle on tired bones and living a simple but authentic life becomes more of a reality.

I wonder sometimes what the world could be like if every weekend was like that.

Wild Solace

"There is something infinitely healing in the repeated refrains of nature," Rachel Carson wrote. "The assurance that dawn comes after night, and spring after winter." I have never felt this so strongly as I do now, waiting for the sun to warm my back. The bottom may drop out of my life, what I trusted may fall away completely, leaving me astonished and shaken. But still, sticky leaves emerge from bud scales that curl off the tree as the sun crosses the sky. Darkness pools and drains away, and the curve of the new moon points to the place the sun will rise again. There is wild comfort in the cycles and the intersecting circles, the rotations and revolutions, the growing and ebbing of this beautiful and strangely trustworthy world.
–Kathleen Dean Moore

I've been thinking a lot this week about solace and how to find it and the healing that so often follows in the midst of grief and sadness. There have been deaths in my community, some the natural conclusion of a long life, some the result of tragic accidents, and some the end of a life that gradually faded away as an illness shouted louder than anything else when it had run its course.

The events in my community in the last few weeks and the resulting thoughts to look for solace makes me think of a time last year, a few days after my grandfather passed away. He was in his mid-90s, so his passing wasn't completely unexpected, but of course, any transition to death brings with it a time of grief.

I took the afternoon off from work the day I got the call that he'd died to walk in the woods, and I hiked to the top of a large rocky outcropping by the river. It was late summer, and the air was heavy with misty humidity. Emotionally, I was experiencing a sense of sadness stemming from empathy for my father, in losing his father, and flashbacks to my grandmother's passing 10 years prior and the sense of loss that I imagine my grandfather must have felt in the days and years that followed as he learned to live alone after 60 years of partnership. These heavy feelings were contrasted by the sounds of the woods breathing, the birds chirping, the winds gently rustling the leaves and little creatures skittering about the forest floor. There was movement, growth and the pulse of life present at every turn.

I sat down on a huge rocky platform at the crest of the trail and let myself feel the sadness that so often accompanies a loss of life, regardless the nature of the death. After a while a butterfly landed on the rock in front of me and fluttered around for a bit; landing, and then flying, and then landing again, but never leaving my general area. Then another one joined in and they kept fluttering around each other and me in a way that I just can't describe with words very well. I had this distinct knowing that these butterflies were somehow my grandparents, somehow symbols of their souls, reunited after 10 years apart in a bodily sense. Their presence was incredibly calming and brought such comfort to a time of gentle grief. They reminded me of the way that life energy can persist even when a physical body passes away—even when a veil of sadness lays overhead. I remember feeling so grateful to those butterflies for finding me and for not leaving right away when they did. I

A Wild Perspective

Toward the end of the summer where I live in Minnesota, gardens are at their peak. The cool loving crops like lettuce and broccoli and peas have given into the heat, but tomatoes, squash, zucchini, beans, berries, melons…all of these are coming into their own as the season matures. As I look out across the field that houses our little patch of abundance, I see a mess of color. There are shades of emerald green as the kale plants start to resemble small palm trees, hues of red and pink as the raspberries and tomatoes start to blush and vibrant yellow squash and cucumber blossoms as the vines get ready to bear round two. There is the orange of a pumpkin just starting to take on its fall jacket and the purple of the tiny eggplants that are relishing the warm humid air.

And punctuating that mess of vibrant color? Weeds.

There are creeping viney weeds snaking around the fence posts and into the raised beds. There are sturdy tree-like weeds interspersed between the pumpkins and bushier weeds mingling with the peppers. There are purple spiney weeds and delicate flower-like weeds and hulking thorny weeds. And there is grass—quack grass and prairie grass and grass that looks like it belongs in the yard, all of it tall and all of it declaring the garden its home of choice.

Early in the season as the seeds that were sown started poking up through the late spring soil, I took care to mulch well in hopes of suppressing some of the inevitable weeds that are part of a garden's life cycle. As the plants came into their own, I found myself clutching a hoe and hunching over rows of tiny carrots and beets, pulling blades of grass one at a time. I put down more mulch and hoed more vigorously. I went out right after the rains so the ground was just right for pulling weeds out by the root. I crossed my Ts and dotted my Is.

And here we are at the end of the summer, and I have a garden full of weeds, once again.

When it became apparent that I was not going to prevail over the weedy conditions without spending every waking hour on weeding related activities, a sense of defeat started to creep in. After all of that, I still failed? What was the point of all of the care and forethought and physical labor? Maybe I just should have been kicking back on the porch with a cocktail, watching the weeds grow instead of spending so much time out in their midst trying to conquer them.

But as the season continues, I find myself looking at the weeds differently. They are a tangled, unorganized, wild and motley crew, to be sure. I didn't want them. But they are thriving. And so are the vegetables and fruits that I did want. Everything out in that garden, planned or not, wild and cultivated, is full of life.

Somewhere along the way, the garden and I came to a sustainable balance. All of that work that I did early in the season was enough when I added acceptance of the things that I didn't want. My efforts prepared the planned garden plants to thrive —even alongside the bits of wild and weedy growth that became their neighbors.

So it is with our human lives. When we can spend energy cultivating our internal growth, whether that comes in the form of reading poetry or practicing yoga or promoting sustainability or fostering forgiveness, we set ourselves up for being able to accept whatever comes into the space that we inhabit. We can thrive when weeds mar our view and perhaps even start to see the beauty in the wildly tangled vines as they mesh with our own. We can let our feelings speak what they need to speak without judging them, and we can learn to find solace in the growth that can happen even in the midst of things that we didn't think we wanted. We can remember that figuring out how to live in the space between what is wild and what is cultivated is an essential component of living in a way that honors the earth and all of the life that wants to exist here.

As the garden season rolls on, I give thanks for the vegetables and herbs and fruits of my labor, and I give thanks for the opportunity to exist alongside the wildness that still thrives even as my human life impacts the earth beyond what I can see in my everyday routine. I remember that hard, honest work and acceptance go hand in hand. And I remember that I want to live in a world where weeds still sometimes get the last word.

Freedom to Roam

I live in "America's Little Sweden." Incorporated in 1894, Lindstrom was first settled by a man named Daniel Lindstrom—he left his homeland of Sweden for the prospect of a new start on American soil in 1853. The water tower is an enormous coffee pot, Dala horses abound, and the Swedish flag is flown with pride. People know how to make lefse, drink Glogg and some even enjoy eating Lutefisk. There is a sister city in Sweden: Tingsryd. You can almost feel the commitment to heritage and the deep bond that gets passed on through families in the air around here, which in modern culture is something that is no longer common. I am not Swedish, though my father's side did come from Norway, so there's a little Nordic blood running through me. At any rate, I can appreciate the sense of belonging to a place that keeps this community's Nordic roots nourished.

Earlier this week I had an unexpected free morning, so I planted some lettuce and carrots in hopes of a fall harvest in a few months and laced up my trail running shoes. Usually when I want to run on trails, I head toward the St. Croix River Valley and all of the interesting rocky outcroppings and winding trails that follow the waterways. But this time, for whatever reason, I decided to go to a park that is right in town. Allemanstratt Wilderness Park is situated within the city limits of

Lindstrom, about a half mile from the main drag, and you can see the Swedish church steeple from its shoreline.

I parked the Jeep and jogged into the cooler air of the dense forest to the songs of the 100 different types of birds who call these woods home. There are huge basswood, maple and oak trees scattered throughout the preserve, which in its entirety is 100+ acres. Some of the trees are upwards of 150 years old and seem to keep watch over this sanctuary, this place that has been set aside to embody the concept of the park's namesake. Alle-manstratt, in Swedish, means "all men's right"—in Scandinavia there's a concept that we could all do well to embrace: Allowing people the freedom to roam. This concept takes the view that all people should be able to freely access wilderness and reap the benefits that come from doing so regularly, as long as it is done with respect for the land and others, without harming the natural environment.

Sometimes I wonder what it would take to get our culture to truly embrace values like the ones that got left behind when people crossed the ocean to the promised land—and the values that informed the indigenous people who already lived here; like being part of nature, rather than separate and living with the land, rather than considering it something to be owned and used for human gain. I can only hope that the slivers of heritage that came along and still embody old world values provide the little bits of space that create the energy the world needs to remember the beauty that is possible. If we can remember that living in a way that allows all creatures the freedom to roam is essential for life to thrive on this planet, maybe the beauty can shine through the scars of the age.

A River Lament

My family and I make our home just down the road from the St. Croix River. There's a public boat landing with some beautiful picnic grounds and a swimming beach about five miles from our house, and it's right on the way to one of our usual grocery store destinations. Basically, it's in the backyard and takes hardly any time or effort to go there.

This past Sunday, Eva and I loaded up a backpack with towels, a yellow bucket, graham bunnies and carrot sticks and headed to the beach area at the landing. Nick met us there after picking up some sandwiches from a local café and we had lunch in the shade of some big cottonwood trees. The temperature was approximately 78 degrees. The sun was shining, and there was a gentle breeze coming off the water. It wasn't crowded. After lunch we walked on the warm soft sand to the water's edge and stood in the refreshingly cold water while Eva played in the sand, making little rivers and islands in between bouts of 'splooshing' into the deeper water. We watched a lady swamp her kayak while getting out of it and smelled a few wafts of cigarette smoke from down the way, but other than that, it was a picture perfect afternoon.

At one point when I was standing knee deep in the water, I turned to take in the view to the south. You can see all the way out of the backwater where the beach is to the main river way, and the view is amazing. There are tree lined banks on either side of the slowly moving water that give way to a broader view of the main channel's high bluffs in the background, their sheer cliffs commanding attention even at a distance. The further you look the more the details blur together into a haze of earthly beauty. You can feel the expansiveness of this wild river flowing on all sides, its energy a calm presence caressing the landscape. And as I stood there, marveling at the awesomeness of this place that is so close to home, I thought,

"Why didn't I come here more often this summer? It's so close. It's so great here. Summer's almost over and I missed so many opportunities to do this."

In the midst of a beautiful moment, I found myself lamenting the fact that I hadn't visited this place more frequently. Instead of simply being in the moment and fully enjoying it, I plucked myself out and started focusing on the experiences that never came into being on all the past summer days when I had chosen to be somewhere else.

So, I'm glad I went to the river this past Sunday, and I'm thankful I caught myself lamenting before I got completely sucked out of relishing in the moment. Because once you notice something like that, you're more likely to notice it again. And again. And again until it dissolves because you aren't lamenting anymore because your default has become focusing on the beauty that is right in front of you, not what's missing around it. We all have a string of moments, and a string of consciousness that weaves them into how we experience life in this human form. I want my experience to be more about relishing in the moment instead of lamenting what might have been missed.

Like Tim Kreider says, "I have this idea that if I could do this, time might hold still for a second, and I would know, for just a moment, what it feels like to be here."

PART THREE

Autumn

Is not this a true autumn day? Just the still melancholy that I love—that makes life and nature harmonize. The birds are consulting about their migrations, the trees are putting on the hectic or the pallid hues of decay, and begin to strew the ground, that one's very footsteps may not disturb the repose of earth and air, while they give us a scent that is a perfect anodyne to the restless spirit. Delicious autumn! My very soul is wedded to it, and if I were a bird I would fly about the earth seeking the successive autumns.

[Letter to Miss Eliot, Oct. 1, 1841] –**George Eliot**

Autumn is defined by transition. Of all the seasons, somehow I feel the sense of transition happening more this time of year as the warmth of summer starts to give way to a new kind of chill in the air. It is a time of lingering abundance as we harvest the fall crops from the garden and preserve them to eat in the winter and spring to follow. There is a sense of anticipation, like there is with spring, but it also holds a tint of melancholy for what is dying. We look forward to respite from the heat and bugs of the summer, but at the same time we ache to hold onto the freedom that comes with being able to just step outside at all hours of the day without shoes. Autumn is chopping wood and chopping vegetables, and it is winding hoses and lingering outside while we can still breathe easy in the above freezing air. Autumn is a last deep breath before the deep sleep of winter, and we savor the days with apple cider, squash soup and the knowledge that our hard work has earned us a rest.

Fading into Stillness

You can feel summer leaving today. The cooler air that whips around my limbs when I go up to the garden to collect the last of the Swiss chard and lingering red tomatoes holds a sense of ownership. It will be sticking around, even with the warmer days that will surely still grace our weeks as the leaves start to turn toward burnt umber and ruby and tangerine. The flock of turkeys is poking around in the field that we didn't till this year, intent on finding whatever treasures turkeys try to find in weedy fields, and their young race around the edges, unhindered by the gusty winds and bleak grey sky. The tomato forest, as dubbed by our toddler, has started to wilt and wither despite the green tomatoes and hopeful blossoms that still remain between the staked patches of vine. The Delicata squash lay exposed, the huge green canopy of their earlier life on the ground around them, interspersed with the squash bugs that insist on making their presence known year after year. Potato plants lie on their sides, waiting to be unearthed, their tubers snug in the soil until we are ready for them, or until the ground freezes, whichever comes first. The inevitable squash vine that grows from the compost heap looks healthy and robust as it stretches its tendrils out over the grass. It must not realize the frost is just likely weeks away. The tiny green pumpkins don't stand a chance.

Such is life in a garden, and in the wild. After a season of cultivation and growth and newness, there comes a season of death and settling in and newness in a different way. The earth is slowing down and making ready the space for stillness and rebuilding that defines winter.

I don't feel quite ready to let the garden go yet—this year was colder than usual, and the plants got a late start. Some didn't pollinate, some didn't grow as we might have hoped they would. I'm just getting in the rhythm of harvesting and sharing the abundance that we have to give. But I don't get to decide. That's the thing about living on the earth—we humans can make all sorts of decisions and plans, but at the end of the day, the earth always gets the last word. There is something soothing in that, even when the earth gives us conditions that we might not want.

Though summer is on its way out for the year, autumn and the stillness that comes with winter are filling in the gaps. As the cold wind blows and the leaves start to fall, I am reminded that there is no renewal without the passing away that punctuates all things in a human life.

Gifts of the Ordinary

Kahlil Gibran once wrote, "We choose our joys and sorrows long before we experience them." There is not a day that goes by that I do not have the opportunity to dwell on 30 seconds of disappointment, or two minutes of worry, or a half hour of wishing I was somewhere else. There is ample challenge, heartache and disappointment to be found in all sorts of places if I want to find those things. The world can be a place of fear and grief, of anguish and loss, or of longing and dashed hopes. When we dwell on what's not right in the world, when we shut out the beauty that persists despite the hardships that pepper our experience, and when we don't open the gift that ordinary offers, the world aches.

I glanced out the front window during a lull halfway through my work day this afternoon and saw my husband swing our daughter up onto his shoulders as they made their way to the garage. The sun was filtering through the newly yellowed leaves on the maple tree, and a gentle breeze was ruffling them, hinting at the coming of autumn. Nick walked slowly up the stone path. Eva rode tall on his shoulders, happily smelling the tiny green blanket that goes with her everywhere and occasionally hooting like an owl. They rounded the corner and were out of my sight lines in about 30 seconds.

It was only 30 seconds, but it was 30 seconds of pure joy.

One tiny slice of joy, added to the other tiny slices that infuse themselves into my consciousness over the course of a day eventually bind together into contentment. Sometimes it takes a while, but at the end of the day, contentment somehow settles into my veins. Those little slices of joy force me to acknowledge that when I look for gifts in the ordinary, when I notice what's right in the world, and when I see the beauty that punctuates every moment, the world gets better. When I choose joy, the world weeps in gratitude, and the ache subsides.

The world wants to get better, and it does when we remember to see beauty where yesterday we saw nothing in the ordinary events that took place. Little bits of the world start to heal when we remember that we are the universe, and the universe is us. The world's ache transmutes into peace when we remember that there is no light without darkness and when we accept the oneness that wants to flow through us.

The world is better when we acknowledge 30 seconds of pure joy on a Monday in September and when we replace worry and longing with the gifts of the ordinary.

Dynamics

I can remember running on a trail that parallels Minnesota Highway 8 down into the St. Croix River Valley last fall and having the distinct feeling that the earth was humming. As I ran alongside the busy highway, the earth's vibration was louder and more vibrant than the constant buzzing of car engines accelerating and braking on the roadway. I remember stopping to touch a rock wall, and feeling its warmth radiate up my arms and into my physical body. I don't recall anymore the specific day, and I don't think that matters—the important thing is that at this moment I am reminded that it happened.

This morning the earth was humming again—she probably has in the days and months that came and went in between now and then, but I didn't think to notice it and write it down until today. This morning's sunrise was a muted pink haze rising out of a darker blue expanse that left a band of light wrapped around the horizon—nothing "spectacular" from many perspectives, but rather full of vibrancy in an understated, calm way. Kind of like a sigh of relief. Once the sun was higher, it radiated what felt like a clean energy into the grass, the water, the birds, the trees . . . everything that was awash in its glow. Sounds were clearer, and little details were easier to notice, like how a robin's wings make a delicate flapping noise when they take off from a branch into flight.

The earth's vibration, her humming, has started to seep into how I perceive things. Sometimes. Maybe more times than not lately. Every so often, a hole of light breaks through the film that tends to cover our senses, and allows more of a fullness in, even if just for a second. The veil still has a tendency to drop back down, but now that I know that it's there and can sense that it is just a thin film over the deep ocean of wholeness and light, it's easier to remember to lift it up again. It seems the humming isn't going to go away.

Sabbath

Yesterday afternoon I didn't do anything. And by "anything" I mean I didn't do anything that I would typically count as "productive." I wasn't at work, and my two year old was napping. I didn't cook dinner, I didn't do the laundry, I didn't work on any projects, I didn't practice yoga, I didn't plan the upcoming weekend. I didn't do any of the things that I usually do when I have an hour or two of time on my hands. Instead I sat at the kitchen table with a glass of wine and looked out the window. The lake was glassy and starting to reflect the late afternoon sunset as dusk claimed ownership of the day's light. The wind of earlier in the day was starting to settle, and the newly fallen leaves lay still, a carpet of yellow and orange and red on the ground. At one point a seagull called out and circled the lake, a spot of bright white against the muted, hazy tones of the landscape. Everything was quiet.

At first I felt that familiar sense of guilt for not using my time to address the next item on the never ending task list—in the fall, it's even longer than usual with the seasonal tasks of gathering firewood, putting up the last of the garden produce, getting the garden ready for winter, raking leaves, winterizing motors, and all the other things that need to happen for a rural household to welcome the winter elements in Minnesota. And there are of course the tasks of daily life always waiting in the wings: Food to prepare, dishes to wash, floors to clean, errands to run. It is all too easy to fall prey to the energy of guilt, self-condemnation and plain old worry.

"What if I'm not ready for what comes next?"

"What if I fail to do what my loved ones expect/need me to do?"

"What if we never finish the list?"

Well. These questions, much like the dreaded "list" could go on for pages. For all the questions that I could come up with, the answer—if I'm really being truthful with myself—is, "So what?" As I was sitting there, looking over the lake and taking in the stillness of the moments as they passed, I was somehow able to see over the *what ifs* into the present. I could see that my taking an hour to just sit still and be wasn't going to lead to the demise of . . . well, anything. Perhaps it will take one more day to get all the apples turned into sauce. Perhaps the leaves will pile up and mat down the grass for more days in a row than would be ideal. Perhaps while I sip my wine, a detail will slide by into oblivion, never to be attended to. Perhaps the world will go on.

I wouldn't want to have day after day of sitting at the kitchen table drinking wine. Things will still need to get accomplished, and I will still be happier when the dishes are clean, I've practiced yoga and the laundry is folded instead of in a heap on the bed. But taking time to just sit and be with the quiet of an afternoon is necessary, too. Most of us need to feel like things are getting done to be content—but we also need to observe time for rest so we can work another day. After all, isn't that what we are working for? To be in the world in a way that invites contentment and peace for all living things? Maybe we need to remember to observe what we are working toward in the first place.

Maybe we need to give ourselves a sabbath, because as Wendell Berry writes, "Sabbath observance invites us to stop. It invites us to rest. It asks us to notice that while we rest, the world continues without our help. It invites us to delight in the world's beauty and abundance."

Peaks and Valleys

Right now my backyard is glowing. It's a mess of yellow and burnt orange with a backdrop of light blue sky and indigo water. It might well be peak color in my little spot on the earth at this very moment. Tomorrow will likely be pretty much the same, but the winds are blowing harder as the days move toward winter. This year's glowing leaves won't be around much longer. Soon enough they'll be part of the forest floor's carpet of dark brown and then they'll get covered in snow. This time of vibrancy is fleeting.

Eva and I went for a hike at a nature preserve yesterday. I got a good workout hauling 35 pounds of small child on my back for most of the walk and on our breaks, Eva had a great time playing in the tall grass and hiding amongst the leaves and rocks and trees of the forest we hiked through. This particular forest is always quite lovely, but yesterday it was astonishingly gorgeous. There's a deep ravine a few miles into the hike, and all we could see as we approached the trail's turn to skirt the drop-off were blazing maple leaves of all hues as far as the eye could see. We were completely surrounded by the energy of the season. We were witnessing the peak.

When we go back next week, it won't look the same. Many of the leaves will have dropped to the ravine's rocky floor, and the sense of walking through a sunbeam will be gone. It will be easy to mourn the passing of another season into dormancy and long for what has already faded away. Many times it seems there is only one way to go from the peak: down.

But perhaps there's another way to look at it. When we look at the seasons of the year in pieces, we see peaks and valleys that are separate from each other. We see times of the year that we like and times that we dread. We see our troubles apart from our triumphs and can't seem to see how things can possibly work out.

Yet if we look at the year as it meshes with all the other years and at the seasons as they flow seamlessly into one another, the picture changes. We can see the wholeness that encompasses the living and the dying, the vibrancy and the fading away. We can see our troubles and our triumphs as part of the same universal breath. We can see that all things are essential to create a beauty that is outside of simple understanding.

Wood Stove

Two weeks ago, a lanky man and his assistant rambled up to the house bearing silver stove pipes and ladders and left two hours later as we gazed at our newly installed wood stove. We got it from a guy across the river that didn't need to have it around and was willing to let it go for a reasonable price that included dropping it off in our garage. After living for all of my adult years without wood heat, having a stove in the middle of the living room feels a bit like returning to home soil after a long journey away. I grew up in a house that was heated exclusively by a wood stove, and I didn't realize how much I'd missed the company of slowly burning logs until I invited them back into my daily life.

And with it has come the task of operating the wood stove—something that Dad always did when I was growing up, and his administrations of which I look back on now wishing I'd paid closer attention. There's a bit of an art to efficiently using a wood stove, and I admire the commitment my parents had to the labor and routine that is required to make such a lifestyle work.

Such a lifestyle requires chopping and splitting wood, curing the wood properly, storing it in a dry place, making sure there's enough kindling to get a fire going, hauling the wood from the storage place into the house every day, clearing the ashes . . . and this is all before you even build a fire. Building the fire requires opening the damper, getting a good small fire burning, and then feeding it larger logs until the temperature and coal bed is hot enough to close the damper again to ensure an efficient use of the fuel. You can adjust the airflow too, for good measure.

As autumn progresses and the air takes on more of a chill, I am thankful for the means to heat part of our home with the wood that grows abundantly in the forested land around our house. Heating with wood is, for us, part of building a life that is centered on simplicity—one of the facets that I believe to be important in living in a sustainable and life-giving way. As we move toward heating more with wood and solar power, we use less fossil fuel and take our support from the corporations that feed on our dependence to those things. We aren't independent of them yet. But every time we make a choice that takes energy from supporting corporations that are based on profit and greed for a few, we put more energy into building a system that is based on truth and abundance for all.

This is not to say that living in a simple way is easy. In some ways, it isn't even simple. At first glance, it seems simpler to flip on the furnace when the temperature dips, rather than going outside to split wood. It is easier to sit down with a cup of coffee and the morning news, instead of using those first moments of the day to start a fire in the stove. The culture we live in today is built on the promotion of buying convenience. Choosing to do something by hand, or the 'hard' way doesn't make sense through the lens of the American Dream.

So why do it?

Because when we choose to live simply—when we see that we have enough, and usually more than enough—we live more fully and are part of the system that allows others to do the same. When we choose inconvenience over doing things the easy or quick way, we offer our work to the benefit of those who don't have the luxury of such a choice. When we choose to accept enough, we return home. We remember what it feels like to love without boundaries and to be content with what we have, whatever it may be.

Footpath

There is a certain rhythm to walking in the woods that can only be achieved by doing it for days at a time. Step after step, rock over rock, root by root, the body and mind sink into a pattern and get worn into the soil. A perspective that gets lost in days spent with computers, cell phones, paved roads and CNN finds a voice when nothing matters other than not tripping over giant cedar roots, avoiding sinking into muddy ground or being able to get warm after a downpour without access to the indoors.

The superior hiking trail is a 240 mile foot path that winds along the coast of Lake Superior and the ridges of the ancient mountains that make up what Minnesotans know as the North Shore. It was born in the mid 1980's and was built and is still maintained exclusively by volunteers. It is a wonderful thing to have close to home—and one to support and use respectfully whenever possible.

This trail is what supported us one October weekend as we wound through groves of cedars, baby maple forests, birch rimmed valleys and stands of stately oaks. All the forest plants were taking on their autumn wardrobe, and the hills were glowing with warm colors. This particular excursion started at a wayside off of Highway 61 where the Caribou River makes its crossing. We dropped the car a ways south and another great invention, the Superior Shuttle, carried us to our starting point.

With a wave to the friendly van driver and hopes that his sunny weather forecast held true, packs were donned and we were off. Ten minutes later we were 300 feet higher, trying to catch the breath that we left at the trailhead while gazing at a torrent of rushing water as the Caribou cascaded over a cedar studded cliff on its way to the shore. Deciding that stopping for a long break ten minutes into a four day trip wasn't wise, we continued... still gaining elevation, shedding layers and readjusting packs that seemed to gain weight every few feet. After what felt like a lot longer than it actually was, we reached our first view of many that invited us to stare out over miles of blazing aspens, groves of maples and sprinklings of pines against a backdrop of a misty Lake Superior. We were reminded why we hike. It's one of the best ways to truly experience creation.

Michael Pollan, author of many nonfiction works about gardening, food and culture, writes of a "wilderness ethic" in his book *Back to Nature*. Part of what he argues is that in modern culture, we have a tendency to either pave over natural areas or put them in protective boundaries that don't allow for much more than observation. There is not much room for partnership in either scenario. We are either destroying natural places or putting them up on pedestals that don't allow humans to be a part of the flow of the natural world.

When we were out on the trail, carrying what we needed for a few days and sleeping in the woods, we did interact with the wilderness—and made a point to respect it, as well. Pollan talks of gardening as the intermediate step between the destruction and sainting of the land, and I see glimpses of that position in the act of hiking through unregulated land. We did our best to leave no trace of our presence, but we took dead wood to burn for warmth, filtered lake water to drink and would have gathered berries to eat had they been in season. The value of interacting with creation—respecting that partnership, and being a part of a truly alive world—is something that everyone can benefit from experiencing. With much of humanity largely removed from nature, it is no wonder it seems like so many can't be bothered with protecting it—they don't know what there is to lose.

This short backpacking trip was a good reminder of what's important in life: Doing things to protect the planet we live on by eating sustainably produced food, driving less, supporting clean energy and living simply while making sure to appreciate and enjoy all that our home planet has to share. Waking up to the tune of dawn spreading fingers of light across the waters of Lake Superior just happens to be a great way to celebrate the abundance of earth and recall why doing what we can to keep the good alive is so crucial.

Cloudy

Most of my days are spent at home. I leave the house every day on foot, to run or ski around the lake, but it's a rarity to find me driving away from the house in a car. I have been working out of a home office for several years now, and the weeks when I don't leave much by car used to feel claustrophobic and unbalanced, like I was missing something or not fully living life. Sometimes that feeling still creeps in, but when I really look at what my days are about, I feel thankful that I don't have to leave if I don't want to. I can just stay and be. I can see my daughter every hour if I want to, and be there to feed her myself all day long. I can see my husband, who graciously has agreed to care for her while I'm down in my office, periodically throughout the day as well. In the spring, summer and fall the garden is just a dirt path away, and my office door can be opened to the breeze, to the filtered sunshine, and to the trees and birds. And in winter I have just a short walk down to the frozen shores of the lake.

Sometimes I let myself get swept up in day to day work "stress"—absorbing the unhappiness of people I talk with, the complaints of my co-workers about how things are done at the office, the general feeling of dissatisfaction with life from so many individuals. It can be extremely challenging to separate one's self from such strong emotions and feelings when they come from so many different people. Fortunately, I interact with people who are feeling great about life, empowered by their decisions and hopeful for the future everyday as well, but for some reason, as fall moves over the landscape and the earth takes on a different energy, the last few weeks have been filled with people who are stuck, depressed, dissatisfied, looking for someone to blame, or are simply sad. This is forcing me to look at these conversations with a different lens and filter what I internalize—it's also forcing me to figure out a way to be a positive influence on everyone I interact with, even if the only communication between us is about something negative or seemingly meaningless to the bigger picture.

At some point in the future, I hope there is no longer a need for my day job as a wellness coach. A world where working to better one's wellness and sense of health and wholeness is not incentivized or part of a "program" would be much preferable to how things are today. A planet full of people who have a sense of awareness, are empowered to do what means something to them and who stand up for what they know to be true and good is something to work toward. I hope we'll get there in my lifetime. But if we don't, spending most of my days at home with the people I love, surrounded by vibrant natural life, and projecting the light that is living inside of me and in this place on earth to everyone I connect with each day will have to do. As a deep ravine is created by drops of water rushing over the same place time and time again, so too is manifesting a shift in how we see our present. One glimmer of light at a time, projected into the cloudiness of the most blustery autumn day will eventually allow a stream of brilliance to shine though.

The Joy of Challenge

Summer has lingered this year, a bit longer than we expected. And by summer I mean nights without a hard freeze—the days have been chilly now for weeks—months really, when looking back at the entire growing season. But the raspberries are still going strong out in the field and the kale and purple cabbage are insistent on thriving even while we remove the spent vines of their neighboring cucumber plants and harvest the last of the onions. The orchard down the road has pumpkins galore, which we are thankful for after a season that produced healthy vines but tiny fruit at our place—fruit that is still trying to grow but will be too late to mature fully before the freeze takes them. Which it likely will tonight, as the temperature dips to 32 degrees.

The natural growing season has come to a close, the hillside above the lake has turned vibrantly yellow and the sun waits longer each day to make an appearance. Autumn and all that it ushers in has descended upon us and the land that we call home, and we bustle around getting our affairs in order before the snow flies. There are boats to put away, motors to winterize, mulch to move and fall tilling to complete. Seed garlic waits in boxes for two weeks post hard freeze when it will go back in the ground for another cycle of life. Leaves are falling fast, the rakes have taken up residence on the front step, and we eat three apples a day. The wood pile grows as the chainsaws dull, and the furnace rumbles to a start and then goes cold. There is work to do, yet. The season has changed, and our energy wanes a bit as the colder air invites cravings for hot tea, blankets and time sitting in front of the wood stove.

So we dig in and do what we can one day at a time. Some things take much longer than expected. Some things probably won't get done at all. Some things will work, and some things will make us groan and hang our heads in defeat. The wood stove will be there when it's time to rest, and we will be grateful we spent the time gathering and piling the wood to burn during the coldest months to come. The outdoor garden tasks will come to a halt soon enough, and we will look for excuses to get outside when the daylight is fleeting during the dark days of waiting that define the Christian season of Advent. We will enjoy jars of tomatoes and bags of frozen raspberries instead of giving into the convenience of picking up a frozen pizza at the local grocery store. The challenges and joys will continue to roll into one, and we will embrace the life that flows through all of it.

A Hidden Wholeness

Five hours west of my little red house, indigenous people from hundreds of tribes around the world have gathered in prayer and protest of the Dakota Access Pipeline. Each week more tribes announce their solidarity with the people of Standing Rock, offering up songs of healing and prayers for the protection of the earth's water. A fellow resident of the St. Croix Valley took her three young daughters to deliver winter supplies to those who have put their regular lives on hold to stand in protection of this essential Missouri River watershed. Others remain committed to oil and the short term promises it makes. Tension builds, and armed police continue to gather in opposition while the mainsteam media remains quiet.

The wind has been blowing the last few days, ushering in the colder air from the north to let us know the time for blossoming and long days of outdoor warmth are over. The forecast for tonight calls for a freeze, and I brought in all of the vegetables and fruits that still lingered in the fields. The water from the hose I used to wash the leeks and potatoes felt like ice, and I moved quickly to get the job done.

There will be a presidential election in one month's time, and America is torn. Some are clear in their choice, while others see no good option. Some have stopped paying attention entirely, taking to the woods to find a version of reality that makes sense.

Some say voting for a third-party is throwing away your vote, while others remind us that thinking like that is why we still only hope for change. At this point, they are all right.

After getting the harvest in, I went back out to the wood-shed to get some of the wood that we'd stacked when the temperature was still 90 degrees. I hurried as I loaded up the wheelbarrow and maneuvered it down to the house to fill the woodbox. Evening this time of year grows dark quicker than I am ready for, and I wanted to be warm and comfortable.

A tropical storm is battering the southeastern Atlantic coast, after causing plenty of destruction in the poverty-stricken island nation of Haiti. Here on U.S. soil, some people flee, while others batten down the hatches to ride out the storm at home. Millions are without power, and there was just a news story on NPR about how the energy grid "still can't withstand nature." People in Haiti mourn and wonder what it would be like to have the choice to flee or stay. And perhaps many don't wonder. There's a Haitian proverb that says "the rocks in the water don't know how the rocks in the sun feel." I don't know what it's like to be without choice. Too many people don't know what it's like to have options.

After coming inside, I made a simple dinner of pasta and just picked broccoli and green beans. While the pasta boiled, I took some small sticks, a bit of paper and some dryer lint, lit a match and watched a small flame start to build. I had to keep the door of the wood stove open for a while to give the fire enough oxygen to burn, and at one point it almost went out when I went back to the kitchen to finish cooking. I came back just in time to blow on the embers and coax a bit of life back into the fire before it went cold. I added some more small sticks and a dry log, and after another few minutes the flames started to dance, and eventually it started to give off heat. I sat down with my dinner and a glass of wine and watched the fire while the wind continued to howl outside.

It's no secret that parts of our world are broken. We know how to fix many of our problems, but we don't know how to let ourselves do what needs to be done to see the solutions through. We are afraid of what could change, and those of us with choices want to be comfortable. We want to watch the news and cluck our tongues at the comedy of politics and post things on Facebook that reflect our views. If we have enough privilege, and if we are being truly honest, we probably worry more about our personal issues than the outcome of the election. If we are in a life situation that puts us in poverty or in a population that endures continual discrimination and violence, perhaps we see hopelessness. Or anger. Or neither because we are focused on surviving another day in a culture that seems intent on chewing us up and spitting us out.

Thomas Merton once wrote "there is in all things a hidden wholeness." Despite the broken parts, the world retains something akin to wholeness. People who were once at war find common ground in protecting that which is sacred to all of life. Pockets of strength build as people who are willing to be brave give voice to those things that don't seem right. People flee or people stay, but whatever their choice (or lack thereof) the disaster brings healing into focus. There is ugliness, hate, and dysfunction in abundance, but so to is there the capacity to tend a small fire in a way that allows it to give comfort when the winds of our time insist on continuing to howl.

Hidden wholeness. Now the trick is to figure out how to make this wholeness we have a little more hospitable for those who don't have embers on which to blow.

Old Beauty

How beautifully leaves grow old.
How full of light and color are their last days.
–JOHN BURROUGHS

I like getting older. I don't know if this will be true when I am 75, but it's true now. I have started to notice a few gray hairs in the last couple years, and I have been excited about each discovery.

Visualizing myself at 75 with a full head of long gray hair doesn't fill me with dread or cause me to strategize about getting an anti-wrinkle cream routine in place now that I am almost 35. I have always been mistaken for someone younger —maybe that is part of the allure of aging. I want to have the life history in me that comes from years of breathing, moving, living, struggling and learning.

The word 'old' comes from an Indo-European word meaning "to grow, nourish." Years of life nourish us and give us history, depth and insight, yet sometimes we think of years as poison instead of nourishment.

Somewhere in the midst of modernization, getting older became a disease, something to be cured or even altogether avoided, if possible. You can't glance through a health or fashion magazine without learning how to look 10 years younger. I haven't watched T.V. much in the last several years, but I would imagine most commercials still encourage striving for a youthful appearance, youthful energy and a youthful outlook on life.

Why is this? What are we so afraid of? Why do people have the tendency to talk to elderly adults as if they were school-age children? In some cultures, growing old is to become wise and respected. Why is it that in our educated, progressive and First World society, being old is to be a burden or something to grieve? Why do we want to stop time or go backward?

Trees are a good example of why growing old is something to cherish. There's a 400-year-old white cedar tree that makes its home along the shore of Lake Superior called "The Witch Tree" or the "Little Spirit Cedar Tree." It is sacred to the Ojibwe people and is a testament to why age should be held as sacred, as well.

The tree is stooped, gnarled, and wind-blown, and it clings to the edge of a cliff. Yet there is beauty and life in every gash, twisted branch, age ring and exposed root, because without those marks, it would be just another cedar tree. The years and marks make it what it is, and the marks and years of human life do the same.

I like getting older because to embrace the passing of another year is to embrace and celebrate who I am and everything—good or not—that goes into my twisted branches, exposed roots and gashes.

Transition Pay

Wednesday this week started as a great day. Eva and I usually spend Wednesday mornings together, and after getting up we went over to a local café that's perched on the banks of a waterfall to meet a friend who's just relocated back to our area. Then we headed south to Stillwater, picked up some things at the food co-op, and stopped in at William Obrien State Park for a hike along the river. The fall colors are tired and past peak, but the landscape remains beautiful with all of its gentle earth tones sprinkled with lingering bits of red, yellow and orange. When we got back home we were both in great spirits.

It's interesting how quickly life can change. Ironically, I read a blog post earlier in the week that said big things usually don't happen when you might imagine—that the bottom of life tends to drop out at 4pm on a Tuesday instead of at a time when you are expecting the worst. Or 2pm on a Wednesday, as it were.

I shouldn't be quite so dramatic, as I am still very much alive and my family is as well. Today, Friday, is also a beautiful day, and I spent the half hour before logging into work on the dock watching a bald eagle and a few ducks move through the mist that was rising off the water. The sun rose slowly in the east as it always does, and this crisp autumn day is getting brighter even as I type these words. Life on the surface looks very similar to how it did two days ago.

So what happened on Wednesday, you ask? After running in the door from our fabulous morning and sitting down at my desk, I got a call as I was dialing into staff meeting that informed me that as of early December, my services are no longer needed at my place of employment. Due to a change in business needs, my position is being eliminated. (At corporations, it's always due to business needs...because let's be honest, in America's business culture, the almighty dollar still tends to win, regardless the compassionate nature of the humans who make the decisions.) There will still be a health coaching department but it will be slightly smaller, and I'm one of the coaches who they didn't choose to keep around. That's tough news to hear after a decade of dedicated service, years of good performance reviews, and being one of the first coaches the place ever hired. Of course, there are people in the world who are trying to make lives in war torn cities, children who are hungry more days than not, and individuals who lose their jobs after 35 years, not a mere ten. But for me, at this moment in my life, losing a job that has become (whether I want to admit it or not) a rather defining part of how I identify myself doesn't feel good.

I've felt burnt out off and on over the years, and I've thought about trying to find a different job periodically—but alongside that, I've been able to work from home, doing something that fits fairly well with my skill set, and provide for my family. I have no idea if I'll be able to find another position that pays me well enough so my husband can continue staying home to care for our young child to keep her out of full-time daycare. I have no idea if I'll be able to find another position that will allow me to telecommute—we live 60 miles outside of the nearest large city, and I just don't have it in me to commute two hours every day to get to an office. My life needs to be close to nature, close to the people I love, and it needs to align with what I value. Finding a job in the city and spending my days getting there and back again doesn't fit. I'm afraid of the next six weeks, the weeks I'm required to work to receive my transition pay, and trying to hold space for and be a positive influence on 10-15 people per day as my own reality shifts in ways that I can't control.

Research shows that autonomy is a key component of finding satisfaction in work, (and life) and right now it feels like my autonomy is being limited. Some choices that I've had over the last ten years are suddenly no longer options. Thinking about finding another job or way to support myself/family while still gainfully employed at a company where I felt very secure is vastly different than thinking about finding another job because I've been let go. I'm afraid of not being able to stay in this house that I've come to love despite its flaws, on this little patch of beautiful land that has been home for the last seven years. I'm afraid that I'll discover I don't really know how to do anything else besides be a corporate health coach, or that I was never very good at it in the first place. It's a classic case of feeling like I'm not enough, even though I know that I am so much more than what I do for a job.

I oscillate between feeling relief that I am being forced to do something different to mourning what I am losing (or might lose). I want to use this turn of events as a way to move more fully into the life that feels right, but I'm terrified of instead moving into a life that is even further away from what I want. In my work I post quotes and memes all the time along the lines of "there is no renewal without the passing away" or "focus on what you have to gain, not what you have to give up" or "everything you go through grows you." I think I still believe in those ways of thinking. Now the trick will be to live like I do.

Krista Tippett, in an interview with the magazine *The Great Discontent* said, "I don't want us to locate the meaningfulness of

Election

A hurricane swept up the east coast last night. It affected a great many people and infrastructure from New York City to the Carolinas to Maine. It sent a record breaking wave into the middle of lower Manhattan. Wall Street was closed for the second day in a row. The presidential campaign had to take a day off. Apparently the earth needed a breather from the constant focus on the illusion of power and negative energy flow that goes on every day, and decided to do a bit of a cleanse.

What if events like hurricanes shook people up enough to re-evaluate how they think and what they project outward every day? What if people paid attention to the voice of the planet instead of the voice of greed, or fear, or anger?

Weeks prior to another presidential election, our phones ring with pleas to vote for the right candidate, our mailboxes are stuffed with wasted paper proclaiming the good news of new jobs and a boosted economy if only we vote for the individual who will stand up for our rights, and too many people hang their hopes on the right outcome of a race that can't be won.

What if "right" isn't even represented on the ballot?

On a morning that ushered in the light with a burst of magenta and tangerine over water that seemed to steam like a hot cup of tea in the brittle autumn air, I wonder what would happen if every person on the earth thought to themselves, "I think I'll try living in a way that honors everything that crosses my path today." What if we voted for peace and love with our whole being all the time?

An old friend of my family used to sign his name with "universal peace now." We've lost touch over the years, so I'm not sure anymore if those words remain part of his signature. I hope they do. Because what if universal peace now came true?

Palpable Joy

Halloween is in two days. Being that this is United States of America, if you've gone into any commercial establishment in the last few weeks, you've been bombarded with pumpkins of all sizes and materials, plastic decor of infinite variety, mountains of orange and black wrapped candy, and enough cheap costuming to clothe the entire country for a year. The holiday season is about to begin in earnest as October gives way to the season of shopping, otherwise known as Thanksgiving and Christmas. Commercialism abounds, we get sucked into the frenzy even if we don't like to shop, and good deals take our attention from being content with what we already have. We eat too much too quickly and have more excuses than usual for why we can't exercise. For many of us, the holidays mean putting on weight, being stressed out, spending too much money and throwing in the towel until January. Often times we are multi-tasking, working late to prepare for a few extra days off or packing frantically to visit the in-laws. We get snippy with our children, our neighbors put up lights that are too bright and we hope the time goes quickly. It doesn't feel like a time of celebration when the culture calls the shots. We forget to be mindful and live in the present.

Bill Kauth, co-author of *Toolbox for a Tribe: How to Build your own Community*, writes about what his group calls a "mindful" Thanksgiving, "After we have circled up, expressed our gratitude, and said what [food item] we brought, we gently agree to support each other in being silent, eating slowly—on very small plates, and even pausing to put the utensil down between bites. Imagine Thanksgiving, with all the special creations with their aroma and flavors, as a wonderful process of sustaining attention on beautiful food. Usually, after a half hour or so, a murmur starts, then it progressively gets louder, and by the time dessert is served we are in full celebration mode. But indeed we are not too full for the desserts as we have been eating very very slowly, with little bites. These are ways of coming into presence with each other. When we do this the joy becomes palpable and our value of long-term community is enhanced. It's easy to see how conscious potluck meals and mindful holidays reflect another tribal value: generosity."

What if a "mindful Thanksgiving" became the norm? What if we all sat down with our friends, families, or in our own company and truly paid attention to the food in front of us? What if we leaned deeply into appreciation for the earth that grew it, the hands that prepared it and the company in which it was shared? What if Thanksgiving and the weeks that follow were about being generous in a way that is much bigger than finding the best present for everyone on our list? What if the holiday season was about cultivating community and living each moment in a way that supports what truly matters to us? What if we could eat slowly and absorb the energy of simply existing, of being nourished and of remembering that gratitude is the foundation of abundance?

I think we need to ask these questions, and then we need to imagine what it would be like to live as if the 'what ifs' were reality. In doing so, we could invite ourselves to be one step closer to living in a more beautiful world. We could learn what palpable joy feels like, instead of just imagining it on the good days. A mindful Thanksgiving? Count me in.

Hope's Light

There are two ways of spreading the light: to be the candle or the mirror that reflects it.
—Edith Wharton

It can be really disheartening to feel surrounded by people who are completely and utterly veiled by the illusions of our time. What does it mean when people talk about TV shows like they are a reality that is worth the energy it takes to form an opinion about? How can it be that people put their hopes for the future on the things that one man or one political party preach to be essential to life? How can people let something as distorted as our current democracy influence their sense of self down to the core? How can people be so afraid that they act out in hate and violence over and over again?

I woke up today, the day after yet another election cycle, and went outside for the usual loop around the lake. It was cloudy, and things looked pretty much the same as they did yesterday and the day before. The air was still, much like the calm after a storm. There was still litter in the ditch, there was still a tractor parked in the middle of a corn field a half mile up the road, and there was still a "vote yes" sign in one of the neighbor's yards. I don't yet know what the outcome of the election was. I hope that more people voted no than yes on certain issues. I hope they will start labeling GMO foods in more states. I hope people can do their best to see the outcomes, whatever they were, and continue about their days in kindness.

Author Charles Eisenstein writes, "We as a society are entering a space between stories, in which everything that had seemed so real, true, right, and permanent comes into doubt.

"What would it take for it [the new story] to embody love, compassion, and interbeing? I see its lineaments in those marginal structures and practices that we call holistic, alternative, regenerative, and restorative. All of them source from empathy, the result of the compassionate inquiry: What is it like to be you?"

So, while the illusions are still as visible and disorienting as ever, there is hope in their midst. There is hope that the choices each individual makes each day mean something and that more and more people continue to choose what's real. There is hope that even if everyday life looks the same on the surface, or for some, even worse, the infinitely more powerful energy of God and the earth is churning to the depths of the universe, celebrating each new being who decides to let themselves be guided by beauty and truth. There is hope in every time people who are on opposing sides see the humanity in each other and let it influence their actions. It may be disheartening to be surrounded by people who continue to let the veil stay locked down, but hope lies in the power of each person who sees the light and decides to live in it.

Elie Wiesel, holocaust survivor and author once wrote, "I speak from experience that even in darkness, it is possible to create light and encourage compassion. There it is: I still believe in man in spite of man."

If Elie Wiesel can still believe humanity is good, well. There might be hope for us yet.

Abundance in Disguise

A lot happens over the course of a single season during the life of a garden. By November, the plants that produced all sorts of good things during the summer have become compost, the fields have been tilled under to mark the close of the growing season, and the leaves on the aspen trees have turned from green to gold. Enough food was grown to eat, to preserve and to give away. Nourishment sprang from the soil and found its way out into the world.

Yet some years I find myself a bit disappointed with the growing season. Like this year: The asparagus didn't produce much, and by the end of summer the patch was completely choked with weeds that I am not sure I'll ever be able to bring myself to tackle. Every time I walk by I think, "man, I hope the patch didn't completely die." The tomatoes, for the second year in a row, were affected by late blight (and got eaten by something) and faded away to nothing before they turned red. The zucchini, so prolific early on, completely succumbed to bugs, and the cucumbers just never took off. The vole got the beets once again, the brussels sprouts are not sprouting, and the carrots are a sorry lot of thin and stubby. There is a lot of failure if failure is what I'm looking for.

But the garden was alive with growth, and it lived for another season, despite challenges. Or perhaps it lives on year after year because of them and the contrast they provide. Sometimes abundance comes in disguise.

Because when I look again, I realize that there are literally thousands of pounds of Purple Viking and German Butterball potatoes in the ground, still waiting to be harvested before the ground freezes solid. Despite the sad state of the heirlooms, the sungold tomatoes fell from the vines like offerings. The pole bean teepee, after a rocky start thanks to some very friendly rabbits, got a second wind and the vines were dripping with slender green goodness until the first frost. The raspberry and blackberry bushes provided a few cups a day all season, and the blueberries did the best they ever have. We froze bag after bag of huge strawberries. I just sorted the garlic for late fall planting, and the bulbs are perfect—every single one that I planted germinated and produced. The basil was bushy, we have more onions and leeks than one family needs, and amidst the sea of grass that went to seed I found five types of winter squash. There was even a watermelon that got bigger than a golf ball. (Until something ate it.)

And the sunflowers. I've been trying to grow huge, ten foot tall sunflowers for years now, and every year has resulted in disappointment. But this year... This year, they reached toward the sky, towering over me every time I walked in to pull a pathetic carrot, reminding me that failure is only a slice of the pie. At the end of the day, there is more abundance to go around than even the hungriest pie lover might want.

Every time I walk by these sunflowers, now drooping and tired after giving life their all, I am reminded that things work. Sure, some things don't. Sometimes it seems like there is death and disappointment around every other corner. But sometimes the sunflowers grow to be ten feet tall, and I remember that all is not lost.

So as we pick the last of the frozen kale bits from the spent stalks and think about making ski tracks around the hay field in the year's first thin snowflakes, we give thanks for abundance in disguise, and we look forward to time to rest in gratitude for what has been and for what is still to be.

To Be Thankful

I think it annoys God if you walk by the color purple
in a field somewhere and don't notice it.
–Alice Walker

It was late fall the year that my daughter was eight months old
and didn't care for the practice of sleeping. The leaves had fall-
en, the days were getting colder by the day, and I was tired. She
wouldn't take a bottle, and I was her only source of food and
often times, comfort. The daylight hours were getting shorter,
and the news headlines were getting more unsettling. Work
days were tiring even without the extra challenge of never
sleeping more than three hours at a time. There was plenty of
anxiety, despair and disappointment to be found in all sorts of
places if I wanted to find those things. I needed something to
remind me of the good that underlays the challenges of life. So
I started forcing myself to acknowledge the little slices of joy,
even in the midst of struggle. I dusted off an old journal and
began writing down those little slices.

Looking back at the entries now, some days sounded pretty
routine: "Witnessing the baby notice the world around her."
Some days included events that will probably never be dupli-
cated: "Watching a black bear cub ramble by my home office

door and scramble up a dead tree and across the ravine in the back." Some days were more challenging: "The contrast provided by people who see the world differently." "The way an unexpected gift of soup from a neighbor can erase the loneliness of a day." Most days celebrated the way a body can move: "Yoga. The way the combination of movement and breath brings focus." And all days were punctuated by the vibrancy of the natural world: "Tangerine skies and evening shadows hinting at possibilities yet to come."

A few years later I still keep the gratitude journal, albeit not as consistently. Sometimes weeks go by before I crack it open and put pen to paper again. But whenever I go back to it, I am reminded that holding the intent to notice the things I am thankful for invites contentment and appreciation for what is to punctuate whatever is going on in my life. The beauty in the world can only grow if we remember to notice it.

When we notice the vibrancy, the good things and the gifts that are sprinkled into our experience and name them, we allow their power to seep into our very being and dictate the lens through which we view the world. Acknowledging those little slices of good shows me that when I look for hints of beauty in the mundane, when I notice what's right in my life, and when I see through a lens of gratitude, the world gets better. Relationships evolve in ways that are good for everyone, aches subside, and even sleepless nights become opportunities to give thanks.

Enough Fear

The autumn that Eva was two years old, she took a header into the stone hearth that surrounds the wood stove. One minute she was racing around the living room squealing in joy, and the next she was face down, her head was bleeding, and she was howling in distress. Nick scooped her up and put pressure on the wound, I grabbed the car keys, and we sped to the ER since it was 8:30pm on a Saturday. We left the garage door wide open, and I was wearing my pajamas. All that mattered at that moment was getting our child to a place of healing.

Eva did just fine through the whole ordeal—she was singing through tears on the way to the hospital and enjoyed a grape sucker and several Little Nemo stickers on the ride home after getting four stitches. As people like to say, kids are resilient. Head wounds look scary and bleed a lot, even when they aren't serious.

In a nutshell, minor childhood injuries tend to be more traumatic for the caregivers.

"Is she going to be ok?"

"How could we have prevented this?"

"What did we do wrong?"

And my favorite,

"What if it happens again?"

The days after the accident we padded the corners of the hearth and had a lot of talks about how important it is to walk in the house and watch where we are going when we do choose to move fast. A week went by, autumn turned to winter, and Eva's stitches came out, barely leaving a mark. The whole thing was a tiny sliver of experience in the big picture of life.

Several months later when Eva was attempting to walk up the stairs by herself—which she could pretty much do by then, albeit slowly—I moved quickly to stand behind her. She shook her head in agitation and said, "No mom, no mom, no mom." She wanted to do it herself, and I was hovering. In my mind, of course, all I saw was a mom ensuring her toddler didn't tumble backwards down wooden stairs. What I saw in that flash of instinct to move right behind her was a bleeding forehead from four months before. My mind went immediately to the hours after returning home from the ER visit, lying in bed with thoughts of "what if it would have been worse?" and "what if it happens again?" swirling in the darkness that tends to amplify things that just need to fade into the background.

I still find myself getting nervous when Eva goes careening around the living room and races by the wood stove, just missing tripping over the hearth by inches. I still stand behind her when she goes up the stairs. I still find my arms reaching out if she starts to lose her balance. And when she races around the living room, sometimes she does trip over things. And she gets back up again. She isn't quite ready to go completely solo on the stairs, but she can make it up on her own just fine without me hovering anxiously in her wake. There are times when she needs to be caught mid fall or picked up from losing her balance. She's still little and she needs her parents to take care of her. But what she doesn't need is a parent who projects the energy of fear into her every waking moment. What she doesn't need is a childhood that is so protected and laced with "what ifs?" that she doesn't learn how to bounce back from challenges, and pain, and undesirable situations. What she doesn't need is a mom who is so afraid of what might happen that she doesn't get to fully experience life and all its contrasts.

I don't totally know how to be that parent yet. (I have a hunch that I'm not the only parent who might feel this way.) Every single day invites a new challenge to find the middle ground between keeping my child safe and letting her figure things out for herself so she can develop the skills she needs to live fully.

Human life is fragile. We know this. Life can change in a blink of an eye and sometimes bad things happen. But despite this fragility, life is best experienced through an energy of curiosity and joy, rather than one punctuated with fear and worry. Children—like all living things—are fragile, resilient, delicate, and sturdy all rolled into one. When they are little, they need protection and care from those who love them. They need concerned attention and hand holding....to a point. But they don't need to grow up in the shadow of fear for what might happen.

They need the freedom to fall down so they can get back up again and thrive.

Lessons of Fall

Here we are once again. In the Midwest, the weather has down-shifted. A month ago the leaves of the maple trees out back were at their peak of orange and yellow vibrancy, and the backyard seemed to glow with a quality of light that is unique to one week of the year. Now as I walk down the steps to the lake, leaves crunch under my feet and the air feels cooler than it has in months. We still haven't had a hard freeze, which is unusual and perhaps yet another sign of a climate that is getting increasingly unpredictable. But regardless the mild weather, the earth is sloughing off her autumn skin and slowing down in preparation for what is to come. Winter's cloak of stillness will be here soon enough.

Though the seasons change every year, sometimes it's easy to forget the lessons we can glean from this age old rhythm of the planet. Each season has its wisdom, and autumn is no exception. There are lessons to be learned if we let the earth teach.

Lesson one: There is beauty in the dying. The folk duo Storyhill sings,

"It's in the color of the trees on the highway
Brilliant with dyin'"

This one is fairly obvious, (who doesn't love a blaze orange tree?) but when we stop and really think about what is going on, we can see deeper into the beautiful offerings that come alongside the passing away. A leaf at the end of its life, when left to ripen on the tree, takes on a beauty that just isn't possible earlier in the season. It only starts to glow after it has surrendered into the next phase of life: making ready for death. In our culture we don't like to talk about death, whether it's the death of a body, the loss of a job, or the end of a dream. We like to get back into our regular routine as soon as possible after whatever has happened instead of feeling grief fully. We make the natural dying process something to fear and postpone for as long as we can, and we like to say things like, "well, all things happen for a reason" and then chin up and move on from the painful ending that we've experienced. But perhaps we miss the beauty when we don't let the natural cycles of a body take their course, or when we don't allow ourselves time to mourn a part of life that is ending. In order to see the beauty in the dying, we need to fully witness, acknowledge, and accept what's going on. There are times to fight for life, or a job, or a dream, to be sure. But there are also times when a life, or a job, or a dream is ready to pass away, unencumbered. A leaf that falls provides nourishment for the forest floor, an idea that dies opens up space for something new to take its place, and a being that dies enters a new phase of the mystery of the soul. Nobody is claiming these things are easy.

And that brings us to lesson two: Letting go doesn't have to be painful. It can be right and good. Of course, there are times when letting go is the hardest thing you'll ever do. Losing a loved one before you are ready to lose them (and who's ever ready, truly?) is challenging beyond words. Being laid off from a job that felt secure feels just plain bad after giving an employer ten years of energy. Yet there are times when we make letting go harder than it needs to be. When we hold on to a season of life that needs to fade, we only create suffering at a time when

Autumn Passing

The lake is like a mirror this morning and has been for the last three days. Thin ice covers the surface, and the images that are reflected, and though they are the same ones as just a month ago, they look different through this new filter. There is a dusting of snow on the ground—just enough to mark the passage into the space between autumn and winter. Things on the surface of life seem to be slogging along as usual, but yesterday as the sun was moving down toward the horizon, the layers of our reality were more apparent than usual. I was out running around the lake and somehow felt lighter than I have in months. I could see the dense, old layer of energy in the clouds that were trying to push down on the light given off by the setting sun, but the light refused to be muted. Even though the sun was starting to move out of direct sight, the positive energy from within it would not be pushed down—it wouldn't give into being controlled. Eventually the sun did set for the day, but it did so on its own terms, a huge red ball of light sinking into the distance. Long after it set, rays of magenta and rose lingered in the cloud cover and bounced off the icy surface of the lake.

Like the sun and its refusal to let its light be dimmed by dense energy, we too have the choice to live in a way that reflects images that are true to who we are and the reality we wish to inhabit. Through the lens of love, light and positive energy, we can choose to live authentically and without fear. We don't have to feel trapped in a life that doesn't speak our truth.

As autumn passes into winter, I am finding that it is important for me to be intentional about keeping the mirror from growing foggy. We can take those images that represent what we want our reality to be; those reflections of how we want to move through our days; and choose to live in them. There is always a choice. I am trying to remember that I can choose to live the reality I want, not somebody else's version.

PART FOUR

Winter

The simplicity of winter has a deep moral. The return of Nature, after such a career of splendor and prodigality, to habits so simple and austere, is not lost either upon the head or the heart. It is the philosopher coming back from the banquet and the wine to a cup of water and a crust of bread.

–JOHN BURROUGHS

A sense of turning inward comes with the onset of winter. Cold weather arrives and we batten down the hatches, fire up the wood stove and spend more time baking and working on projects inside. The cross country skis and ice skates come out in preparation for the snow and ice, and there is opportunity to embrace new possibilities. Venturing outside is a welcome change from too much time indoors, and the silence of a snowy forest is as palpable as the sensation of icy air on exposed skin. Every sound feels like it's cradled in feathers as a new sense of muted wonder takes hold. Winter at its best is peeling off your frosty winter coat after some frigid laps around the frozen pond and discovering that someone built a fire in the wood stove while you were outside. It's sitting down at the kitchen table to journal by candlelight in the predawn darkness while the coffee perks. It is warm blankets, fresh bread straight from the oven, steaming mugs, crackling fires, good books, children whispering in a corner, acoustic guitar music and conversations that mean something. These, for me, are the best of winter, and I make a point to remember that each season is what I make of it.

Shocked by the Possible

The first real snowfall of a newly cold season is always a little shocking. Especially when it seems to come out of nowhere on the tails of an Alaskan typhoon. One day the ground is brown and dry, the sun is out and the corn is still waiting to be harvested . . . and then next everything is blindingly white, the horizon is grey with snow-filled clouds and the memory of dry ground grows more distant with each glance out the window. Piles and drifts of snow now cover every inch of the ground, buildings, trees and roads.

This morning as it was still coming down, I went out into the garden and woods behind the house on snowshoes. It was eerily quiet, all sounds muted by the layer of new snow. Even though we live out-of-town, cars can still usually be heard going by on the busier roads, planes occasionally fly overhead and people are out and about. Not so today—it was silent, except for the thud from piles of snow that sometimes fell to the ground from the trees, or a bird calling from an unseen perch. The only sounds I could hear were from the earth herself, relishing in the respite from human frenzy, enjoying the deep stillness, if even for just a short while. The silence was eventually broken by a tow truck that slipped off the road and into the ditch, its lights flashing in the white expanse, but even the harsh sounds of metal clanging were overshadowed by the sense of calm.

Perhaps this sense of stillness and peace is the earth's way of telling us to stop. To rest. To slow the constant push to move on to the next thing. There are so many who may never stop to take in what is actually happening in the world. To rest. To be with what is happening "right now" in their lives. I suppose that is their choice, and one that I have to accept. I've been that person, too, and will probably be again. Even on my best days, I've never been able to impact someone else's free will. And sometimes I forget that I have my own to do with what I wish. That's ok as long as I remember more than I forget. Those 'other' people? They are okay, too, and they can exist how they need to exist. I can choose to acknowledge the way of stillness and peace, even while walking beside those who do not. I can be tranquil even in the midst of my own inner typhoons when they start to swirl—every storm has an eye, after all, one that provides space to remember and grab onto that peace to ride out the next wave.

So I can embrace the stillness that lives inside and give thanks for it when it is visible outside. I can make peace with what is, what has been and what will be. And above all, as Rumi celebrates, I can "Come out from the circle of time and into the circle of love."

I can be shocked by what's possible when I live that way.

Giving Up the Gym

Usually my days start by rolling out of bed, putting the coffee on and lacing up my running shoes. I run the same loop around the tiny lake that is a center point for my rural neighborhood most days in the spring, summer and fall. Once the lake freezes, running gets replaced by cross country skiing or snowshoeing or—on bitterly cold or otherwise miserable weather days – yoga by a window. (After all, even for the hardiest of souls, sometimes facing the elements just seems like a foolish idea.) I find that being active outside of four walls is essential to keeping me balanced and feeds my commitment to doing what I can to care for the wildness that's left in the world. Active time outside to reconnect with the energy of my natural surroundings helps keep me grounded in reality.

The other day it occurred to me that I haven't been inside a gym since the fall of 2010. Back then I was a member of one of those 24 hour fitness places that have popped up everywhere in America, and I found myself on an elliptical trainer or treadmill 4-5 times per week in a dark little building in my community's downtown area. Rewind six more years and you would have found me in a gym every day. While in college, I studied Health and Wellness, did multiple internships at fitness centers and got certified through the National Academy of Sports Medicine as a personal trainer. My first 'real' job out of school was at LifeTime Fitness, which is now a giant in the health club industry. My second 'real' job was at another fitness center that specialized in supporting people with disabilities. In short, indoor fitness punctuated my professional life. And since I was working at a gym, I exercised at a gym, too. It made sense.

But as I transitioned out of a gym-based personal trainer role and started working from a home office, spending time at a fitness facility started to make less sense. I didn't wake up one morning and say "today is my last day ever in a gym" — The lack of a gym in my routine just evolved out of what my life was asking for. It was asking for more sustainability, and using electricity to power a treadmill so I could get a workout started to feel inconsistent with what I value. It was asking for more beauty, and though I think beauty can be found anywhere, I was having a hard time noticing it between the weight stacks. It was asking for more light, and the hum of industrial grade fluorescent bulbs wasn't giving enough. Winters where I live in Minnesota can be really harsh and long, so on one hand, having access to a gym in this part of the world seems essential. But looking through a lens that points out what is best for the earth and what is best for the part of me that craves living in a way that feels organic? A gym just stopped fitting into what mattered.

While I still regularly offer support and guidance to others who find fitness centers to be central to their success, I am more content when I don't use one myself. Not everyone has regular access to areas that support outdoor exercise, but I am fortunate to live in a place that has abundant trails, safe back roads, lakes and rivers to explore. Everyone has a different physical activity equation that works best for their current life situation. I have seen firsthand how fitness facilities can invite benefits to a huge range of individuals, and truth be told, gyms have benefited me, too. But right now, and in the last several years, what has served my well-being best is finding ways to move surrounded by nothing but earth, sky and fresh air, regardless of how cold that air might be.

Scandinavian Wisdom

"Lagom" is a Swedish word that I discovered a few years ago. It means "enough, but not too much" and says a lot about Swedish culture and lifestyle. The idea of *lagom* allows more than enough for bare necessity while still adhering to limits. Basically, it means just the right amount and recognizes that just the right amount is different for everyone and is always changing. I'm still working out how to use the word in a daily life that isn't based in Sweden.

But today I'm not going to ponder Sweden or *lagom*. I want to say more about another Scandinavian word, but this time one that comes from the Danes. The word is "Hygge" and according to Jim Walsh, "..it describes an intentional chilling out of the spirit as a way to harmonize with—not combat or stave off—the darkness of winter, and an intentional meditative time created out of the much-maligned but potentially fruitful malady we desperately call cabin fever."

And according to Helen Dyrbye, "It is the art of creating intimacy: a sense of comradeship, conviviality and contentment rolled into one."

Minnesota has a climate not so different from the one that birthed this concept of *hygge* in Denmark. Days this time of year—the ones that cozy up to the winter solstice—are short. And even when temperatures are above average often they are still below freezing. I enjoy winter and all the activities like skiing and ice skating and sledding that are possible when the temperature drops—but I'm not immune to the waning daylight and cold extremities that come with the winter days. From December to March, northern mid-western America—even for those who love to be outside in the snow—can feel bleak.

And that is where *hygge* comes in. I experience *hygge* when I go out into the cold evening air to get a few more logs for the fire and come back in to find my husband has put on some Finnish folk music and Eva is coloring while wrapped a blanket in front of the woodstove. I experience *hygge* when we are invited to a neighbor's house for a potluck on a frigid night and everyone who enters radiates a sense of gratitude upon walking through the front door into the warm kitchen. I experience *hygge* in warm mugs, the smell of woodsmoke on the path to the house, and thawing out after ice skating across the lake and back again. It's in homemade bread rising, the glow of candles at the start and close of a day, the gift of a handmade scarf, and the dance of flames in the woodstove while sipping wine and talking about things that matter.

Hygge comes into being when we can find ways to embrace the dark, to nurture relationships, and to find those parts of ourselves that can be satisfied with the moments just as they are. It is taking the time to slow down and savor all the things that lead to a sense of contentment, coziness and community building. It is about becoming intimate with what truly invites a sense of joy and satisfaction. Americans have ways to go when it comes to mastering the art of "savoring," but when we can figure it out and teach our children to practice it as well, I think we'll be onto something. Kind of like the Danes are. And the Swedes.

I guess Scandinavians know their stuff when it comes to simplicity and making the best of it. *Skål!*

Quiet

The afternoon is still. The sky is a dull gray expanse in all directions. The rustle of a jacket and slice of a ski over packed snow breaks the eerie calm. I am at Wild River State park, and there is no one here but a gruff looking man filling the fuel tank outside the trail center and a park ranger in the hut by the entrance. And me, arriving after a morning of office work for a few hours on the trails before going back to resume my post at a desk the rest of the evening.

I head south (at least in my head it's south, but this park tends to mess with my sense of direction) away from the abandoned, yet cozy with a fire going in the wood stove, trail center and try to get my skiing legs back after months of dry land ambulation. For a while it's like I'm an elderly person shuffling along, just waiting for a misstep and resulting broken hip, but after a few hundred yards things get a bit better. "Oh yes . . . remember to move the arms like this and push off like this . . . ."

After a few minutes of zinging along I am confident enough to take in the view I am skiing through. There are trees everywhere: pines and oaks mostly, thick through this section. I have been here before, but in the summer when people ride bikes and drag unwilling children on short hikes. In the winter, covered with twelve inches of snow, it is a different world. There are no people and almost no sounds when I stop moving, save the squirrels and a few birds. In most parks within 60 miles to the city, traffic can still be heard to some extent. Not here, at least not where I am. It is simply quiet, and quiet like it can only be when the sounds of nature are muted by snowfall.

There used to be huge white pines where I am skiing. There's a display alongside the trail illustrating how large they were, as well as how hard to haul out once the loggers took them down. This forest was a different place 100 years ago—it's just a baby compared to what it once was, before logging took it and the ancient trees were gradually replaced by the current tenants. There are still a few white pines here, up on a ridge fittingly called "white pine ridge". They are striking as you round the bend from the nature center and look out over a ravine and into the stand. Taller than all of the others, the woods feel different somehow when they come into view. In the winter they are stark contrast to the deciduous trees that surround them, vibrant green amidst smoky grays and browns and the white of the snow.

I ski past this most enchanted section of forest, more than once almost face-planting due to gazing at the view instead of paying attention to the act of cross country skiing. There are a few leaves on the trail here, and this proves dicey at times, especially when sailing down a curvy hill. One well-placed leaf in the track can put a hard stop to any momentum that has been building. Luckily, I avoid crashing and before I really want to be done am back at the trail center. However, from past experience, I tell myself that it's better not to overextend one's self early on in the ski season, or the hip flexors will pay the price a few days later.

I coast up to the building, notice that the Jeep is still the lone car in the lot and take off my skis for the day. A warm stove waits inside, and I have two hours before I need to be somewhere else. All in all, a superb winter Monday afternoon.

Two Weeks

The last fourteen days have been punctuated by putting on ski boots, grabbing poles and skate skis and walking out the sliding office door down the rickety stairs to the dock to access the lake. It takes twelve minutes to skate ski one loop, and going around three times makes for a decent workout. Skiing these loops has been an opportunity to notice the stillness of the snow and the way it shimmers in the bright sun and keeps record of other creatures that went the same way. It has been time to watch the sun come up in a tangerine haze, and to see it sink behind the trees at dusk, covering the lake in a pink shadow at the close of the day. It has been time to focus on movement and feeling alive, time to notice the birds and how the brittle cattails stir in the westerly breeze. It has been time for being outside of time, for just being.

I am grateful for these past two weeks because the conditions were just right for skating, which is rare and doesn't happen often. I am grateful for these two weeks because they also included many long, challenging nights of being up for hours with a child that just wouldn't sleep. I am grateful for these past two weeks because a number of people that I love are going through a difficult period and are struggling to stay grounded. I am grateful for these two weeks because they have reminded me why I live where I do, how much I love my family, and that even when things don't play out as I might prefer and the days get rough around the edges, the beauty of a sunrise over frozen water or the shriek of a hawk circling overhead helps bring things back into focus.

I won't ski today because it's raining, the snow is gone, and the lake is a puddle. I will miss skiing the loop, but I am grateful for the moisture. I am grateful for the patterns that the puddles make on the lake, and for the new ice that will form once the temperature drops again. I am grateful for a day to rest and notice the beauty of the earth in another way. I am grateful that everyone slept last night and for the sunrise, even though we couldn't see it through the misty conditions. I don't know what the next fourteen days will be punctuated by, but whatever comes, I do know that the sun will keep rising, I will keep living in the present, and I will be grateful for the opportunity to be.

Beyond the Sunrise

This morning the sunrise was, simply put, amazing. As I walked into the kitchen in the darkness of predawn, a fuchsia band of light started creeping up above the tree line across the lake. Outlined by the lingering shadows of night, it was like a slice of raw energy piercing the horizon. The fuchsia band continued to grow as morning got older, eventually casting rose colored reflections onto the visible ice on the lake, and provided a brilliant marmalade and pink backdrop for the skeleton trees that stretch up from the shoreline. The morning was awash with vibrant colors, the power of untamed beauty and an energy that permeated deep into something much broader than the rising sun. I could feel down to the earth's core of peace and joy.

And then it was done. By the time the sun was ready to peek out from the horizon, the clouds were heavy enough to obscure the actual sun rising into view. The colors faded, and the lake and shoreline returned to the usual gray and white, and the skeleton trees faded into the background.

You might say that life lately is like this morning's sunrise. We recognize little glimmers of such joy, and see such potential for beauty and love to engulf all of creation from time to time… and then the day unfolds as usual, unremarkable, tired. What do we do with the unremarkable times? How do we remember the vibrancy that underlies all form when slogging through a tedious task at work or home? How do we see the beauty that is still there, behind the cloud cover?

We use our choices and freedom as humanity to make our world reflect the backdrop that is real. We accept nothing less than amazing, and on days when the clouds are thick, we draw on our internal being, our divine nature, and our power as co-creators to cast positive, brilliant energy into each moment as the present continues to unfold.

Ski Fairy

I woke up this morning feeling...off. Not terrible. But not good either. Definitely not good enough to feel positive about the trajectory of the day. After a weekend of great conversation, cozy fires, and time away from a computer, a day when office work was back on the agenda seemed like a practical joke of the meanest sort.

How could it be time to spend another day sitting in front of the computer, making phone calls and working on things that seem so irrelevant to the grand scheme of what matters in the world? And how could it still be 15 below zero at 8am for the fourth week in a row? I was unsettled, and it seemed like interacting with anything even slightly undesirable would cause me to slip into an all-day melancholy. As I was resigning myself to a day spent tapping a keyboard, I saw the sun through the window and noticed the sparkle of the snow against the skeleton trees of the lake's shoreline. But the frigid temperature and the schedule of my afternoon overshadowed the beauty that I usually see in those things. I felt myself slipping into a haze of wanting something different. I felt like someone who doesn't like winter and someone who dreads the work week.

So I went outside. Instead of letting myself simmer in that haze of wanting, I put on my ski boots and prepared myself for a slow, face freezing loop around the perimeter of the lake through knee deep snow. I wasn't looking forward to it, but I know enough about health and wellness to understand that getting some fresh air and exercise can boost one's mood—and enough about motivation to know that you don't have to feel motivated to do something. Sometimes you just have to do it. So I went outside, down the snow crusted steps to the snow crusted dock and started skiing through the snow crusted snow drifts.

And then I noticed something.

As I glanced to my right, I noticed something that looked strangely similar to a track that you might see at a state park after the trail groomer has rumbled by.

Some kind soul had taken it upon themselves to groom a Nordic ski loop on our little private lake. It was like a fairy had come by and sprinkled magic dust over the lake, turning it into a paradise instead of a frozen wasteland. Granted, it wasn't perfect. There were washed out sections, and it wasn't always as straight as you might see in a dedicated trail system, but there they were: A set of groomed cross country ski tracks right outside my back door. For someone who checks the grooming conditions at the state parks a bit obsessively this time of year, this was reason for celebration.

It was also enough to snap me out of my melancholy stupor and remind me of all the things that are worth celebrating during the days that I spend here on this earth, despite work computers, endless phone calls and frigid temperatures that refuse to release their icy grasp. There will surely be days in the future when I feel off balance or in want of something different. But there will also surely be little things—like an unexpected ski track—that punctuate even the dreariest of days with yet another detail that makes life worth celebrating.

It's nice to remember why I like winter. It's nice to remember that I don't have to let waking up on the wrong side of the bed, the news media and a task list that I'm not looking forward to color my whole day black. And it's nice to notice the beauty that pierces the cold with a single act of thoughtfulness.

I don't always want to settle for just good enough. But I do want to remember that being ok with good enough is part of what makes a life worth living.

Here's hoping the ski track lasts for a while.

The Dark

Darkness falls early this time of year. By 4:32pm in December, the sun has left the day behind and night reigns until dawn of the next day. Sometimes people say it's darkest right before the sun starts to rise again with the morning—this may or may not be true, but either way, the hours prior to sunrise can be cold and feel emptier and more hollow than any other time.

Today a Christmas program was a large part of our church service, and the building was packed with elementary kids, parents, sisters, brothers, aunts, grandpas, uncles, great grandmothers and countless more. There were smiles, laughter, mistakes and screeching microphones in the midst of a community wrapped up in expectation and joy as the season of Advent moves closer to Christmas with each breath.

Across the country, a small town in the east also probably had Christmas programs planned and churches packed with children, parents, uncles, grandmas, sisters, brothers and great grandpas. In those buildings, there were probably faces of anguish, questions of why and waves of grief in the wake of a senseless act that took 27 souls far too soon for their families. People at these services probably have a hard time remembering expectation and joy as the season of Advent moves closer to Christmas with each breath.

What makes the promise of another Advent matter to a weeping mother, or a sister who finds herself a newly only child? What can someone five states away do to help someone who doesn't know how to live in the world anymore? Where is the light, the peace of God, the love and oneness of all things... where is it in the darkness of violence, of hate, of intolerance?

These questions aren't easily answered, and maybe the answers can't even be comprehended by a human mind, but there is one thing that I do know. I know that hope can be found in even the darkest of places, and that even when expectation and joy are pushed under the veil, the light and love of God will not go out.

For those who are far away, snug in a community that only hears of these horrible events on the news? We can turn off the news—we don't have to engage with the sensationalism of what happened, and we don't have to let the media tell us about the individual involved or listen to account after account of what happened. We can remember the children and teachers who were taken from their families, and project light and love into the void that they left. We can remember that their souls are now helping to shine light into all the dark places that still linger on the earth.

Darkness falls early this time of year. And though recent events can leave us feeling hollow and empty, we can look to a new day, the brilliance of the dawn after a deep sleep, and we can welcome the love and light that might shine brighter than we expect in the days to come.

Waiting for the Sacred

It is two weeks into the last month of the calendar year, and across much of the continental United States it feels like winter has arrived in full. The solstice—the official turn of the season—is just a week away: The end and the beginning. Those of a Christian faith wait in hopeful expectation for the promise of light to arrive on Christmas as another season of advent progresses. The sun continues to rise and set in an ancient rhythm. Undertones of anger and injustice remain alive and well in too many places. Living creatures die at the hands of other living creatures, for reasons that are as wide ranging as the stars even as they mirror patterns that have repeated for generations. Traffic moves across the globe, we continue to consume, and our footprints seem to go deeper by the day. Yet I hold onto expectations and hope that something better will reveal itself in a way that can be recognized.

Professor Debra Dean Murphy writes, "'Waiting' works if you live in a world where you know that a little more patience generally would do you good. 'Hopeful expectation' has a pleasant enough sound if your life is going reasonably well at the moment. . . .

"What does 'hopeful expectation' sound like, look like in places where justice has long been delayed, meaning, of course, that justice has been denied?

Hope is not wishful thinking; it is risk and action and the courage to undertake both.

But . . . it is also vulnerability and a willingness to walk alongside those whose hopes have been crushed."

How can we look at our expectations in the midst of crushed hopes and see that there is still, somehow, a sacred energy in our individual waiting, in our lonely anticipation, and in the unknowns that pepper our psyche? How can we honor those whose hope is buried under the rubble of someone else's choices? How can we accept without giving in to the status quo? How can we listen in a way that reminds us of what is possible? I can't claim to know the answers to these questions. I don't know that anyone can.

And meanwhile, the hours, the minutes, and the days continue to tick by. It's business as usual.

Or maybe it's not.

In every moment of each hour, in every day of every year— with each breath in every passing second—we have the power to see that our inner energy is itself sacred. We can let it flood outward into the earth and all of humanity and creation. We can choose to notice this sacredness that surrounds everything, and we can let it inform the way that we live out our days. We can let it be the guide and the hope when it feels like there is nothing else to look toward. We can let it teach us to respond instead of letting ourselves react to the injustice, the hurt, the anger and the oppression that permeates our world.

"May he not come suddenly and find you sleeping. What I say to you, I say to all: 'Watch!'" (Mark 13: 36)

We can stay awake. It isn't easy, but we can keep trying to watch and be present to what's going on. We can be sacred, and we can know that our expectations are truth, though that truth might look different than we anticipated. It might be harder than we thought to stay awake. We can listen and let the ancient become new again, just like the sun that rises and sets. We can step outside the illusions of our time to be in what we know is real. And we can stand in solidarity with those who are experiencing hardship and keep our eyes open to what we are being called to do in the world.

Declining Baselines

Environmental activist Derrick Jensen writes, "This phenomenon is something we all encounter daily, even if some of us rarely notice it. It happens often enough to have a name: declining baselines. The phrase describes the process of becoming accustomed to and accepting as normal worsening conditions. Along with normalization can come a forgetting that things were not always this way. And this can lead to further acceptance and further normalization, which leads to further amnesia, and so on."

His example of this phenomenon is watching a pair of foxes poke around his forest cabin, as well as a raccoon, another visit from a fox and a black bear, all in one evening. He recalls being enchanted in the moment of witnessing this conglomeration of non-human life thriving outside his door, and rightly so. There is always room for celebration and enchantment when we see beautiful things like life thriving in nature. And then the next day he remembered that he once read that people in his area, before the Europeans settled it, typically saw a grizzly bear every 15 minutes.

Declining baselines.

For many of us it is normal to encounter only birds and squirrels over the course of weeks or even months. Regular interaction with wildlife, for multitudes of the population, is no longer normal. Now the unusual thing is to see a wolf or a bear in the wild.

I grew up in a part of the world that sees hard, long, cold and windy winters. It snows in November and doesn't start to green up again until May. But when I look back at the years my daughter, age three, has been alive, this is no longer the case. We still get snow, and cold and wind, to be sure. But we also regularly get 50 degrees in December and this year we didn't get a hard freeze until two weeks before Thanksgiving.

Declining baselines.

I often wonder what the weather patterns will be like when Eva is an adult. Will she remember seasons as I do? Or will her baseline be completely different?

And finally this week the world has witnessed once again an act of violence and terror that is hard to fathom for those who are on the other side of the ocean. Life was lost, fear is rampant and the world seems further from peace than ever before. I can't help but see this too as a decline in what we see as normal. In the last 20 years acts of unthinkable violence against myriad groups across the world have become, as much as I hate to type the words, common. It will never be "normal" to inflict harm on another human being, but it has somehow become common. Eva will never know a world where September 11 didn't happen and she will probably always have to take her shoes off to fly on a commercial airplane. She will never know a world where the word "terrorist" and "refugee" weren't once a regular part of dinner conversations all over the world.

The world events that we hear about over all forms of media, and those events that even sometimes personally affect us, still seem unthinkable to me. But I've noticed that I'm no longer surprised when they happen.

Declining baselines.

Jensen goes on to say, in his standard "no sugar coating it" way, "Do not go numb in the face of this data. Do not turn away. I want you to feel the pain. Keep it like a coal inside your coat, a coal that burns and burns. I want all of us to do this, because we should all want the pain of injustice to stop. We should want this pain to stop not because we get used to it and it just doesn't bother us anymore, but because we stop the injustices and destruction that are causing the pain in the first place. I want us to feel how awful the destruction is, and then act from this feeling."

And he makes two promises: Letting ourselves feel this pain won't kill us. But numbing ourselves while continuing to avoid it surely will.

In response to the recent attacks in Paris, Islam scholar Omid Safi wrote, "In the afternoon I took my children out for a long, slow walk in the woods. We took time to reflect on the trees, the light, the fallen leaves. In the midst of grief, there is still time to hold a friend's hand, to hold a beloved in the heart, and go for a gentle stroll.

"I don't have the answers.[…] But I do know this: at the end of the day, love and unity will have the victory. If we are to get there, we have to remain fully human.

"If we close our hearts to love, to each other, to nature… we have already lost. There is grief in the city of light, and in so many cities of light. But in the midst of the grief, in the late hour of Fall, a beauty lingers. Love shall have the victory at the end of days. Let us welcome light into our hearts, and be agents of healing."

I can only hope that by allowing our grief, our confusion, and our love for the earth and each other to be truly felt…I can only hope that can be enough for this sometimes very broken world to start to heal.

Baselines can be slippery. We best hold onto the ones that remind us what being human is supposed to feel like.

These Gray Days

It's been overcast and rainy for the last six days here in Minnesota. Today I went outside shortly after waking to stand on the dock. I could hear the resident beaver chomping on some old lily pads as he poked around in the reeds, and the robins that are still here, even though it's December, were chirping in the bare tree branches. A bright green kayak was resting on the neighbor's dock, now put away for the winter months, and a hawk circled far above my head, piercing the air once with its call. The lake was utterly still, and the reflection of the skeleton trees along the shoreline stared back at me like a challenge to discern what is real and what is an illusion.

The gray days have started to take a toll, I think. Overly warm weather for this time of the year in combination with constant dampness, and a landscape that seems discontent with its conditions is a combination challenging even for the cheeriest of souls. Some kind of rodent ate part of a shoe that I'd left on the back deck last night, the cream that I wanted to put in my coffee was already sour when I opened the bottle, and our car is in the shop for the second time in a month. And this week ends with the last day of work at a job that I didn't choose to leave, after ten years of service. Life feels hard, more often than not right now. There is much to lament, if lamenting is what I want to do.

But then I look to my right, and I see love and support in the form of flowers that my spouse brought home last night because he could tell I was having a tough week. I can hear joy in the form of my four year old upstairs chattering about something that is exciting to a four year old. Each time I look at my work email, I find a new message from a colleague wishing me well as I wrap things up and the opportunity to appreciate a kind word of acknowledgement. I take a sip of hot coffee, and it's still satisfying, even without the cream. Being down a car today means that perhaps I can wait until next week to ship my computer back to the corporate office and instead use my last evenings "after work" to relax by the fire. The rodent who ate part of my shoe hopefully got the satisfaction he needed from his nibbling. At any rate, I can still wear the shoe, and it was a mud shoe anyway.

Blogger David Cain might call this a way of practicing "radical gratitude:" "Radical gratitude is simply a way of challenging our initial feeling that a new development is wholly bad and that our moping and anger is justified, exploring instead what might also good about it."

The lake remains still and the sky overcast and gray. The reflection of the skeleton trees remains, and the challenge with it. But there is goodness to be found despite the dreariness of the days. In the reflection of the trees I can see hints of movement. I can see the illusion start to dissipate even as parts of the reflection remain visible, and I'm reminded that even gray days provide moments for which to give thanks. As Mary Oliver once wrote, "Someone I loved once gave me a box full of darkness. It took me years to understand that this too, was a gift."

Active Waiting

It's mid-December. Right now the temperature outside is about 40 degrees at 6pm on a Monday evening. The lake iced up at the end of November like usual, and then it rained and the ice melted. Every day it seems the sky is gray and heavy with rain, and the ground is soggy. I have seen three mosquitoes in the last week. Our seasonal stream, the one that only runs during the spring melt, is freely flowing and has been for a few weeks now. The geese are still here. The silver maple looks like it wants to bud and we hope it doesn't. I could go out to the garden and plant more garlic if I wanted to since the ground is no longer frozen. Our skis are in storage, and it's hard to believe that Christmas is next week. We are waiting for the cold and snow that illustrate the Christmas season we are used to.

When you look at what's going on in the world, it seems to be crumbling, or spinning out of control, or making progress, depending on what you value. Politics seem more like a comedy show every time you turn on the news, world leaders still get together behind closed doors to decide the fates of Indigenous people and the loudest voice gets to make the decision at the end of the day.

The climate talks just ended in Paris, the same Paris that weathered so much public violence just weeks before the talks started. Politicians argued over how to address the changing climate, and if you squint at the agreement that resulted from all of those meetings, a hopeful outcome squeaked out at the end. World leaders agreed to act. Time will tell if those promises actually come into being, as there was no binding language in the agreement that was passed. We'll have to rely on their word and hope the agendas of big oil and industrial ag change. We'll have to hope that people are willing to act and think differently and embrace ways of doing things that they thought they never would.

Seems hopeless, right? It's easy to get sucked into thinking that nothing will ever change, that it's all for show. World leaders can talk and agree on things until the cows come home, and the cows might never show up. We the people might say we want to contribute to the healing of the world, but then it gets hard and it's easy to just keep on doing what we are used to doing. Activism and protests and chaining ourselves to trees will buy us time, but the most seasoned environmentalists know that it's not enough. It's never enough.

And right now, in the midst of all of the chaos that is spread to the four corners of the Earth, it's also Advent, the Christian season of waiting. And it certainly feels like we are waiting, regardless of our religious inclinations. Waiting for something to shift, for someone to pass the bill that will make our lives better. Waiting for the other shoe to drop, for the shit to hit the fan. Waiting for mom to get through treatment, for dad to agree to be moved into assisted living. Waiting for that big presentation to be over, for vacation to finally arrive. Waiting for everyone who doesn't agree with our point of view to finally see the light.

We don't have to wait in despair, however. We don't have to wait for someone to swoop in and save us. We don't have to let the unknowns and the violence and the desecration of our lands plunge us into doing nothing and wringing our hands while we wait. We can be active in our waiting. We can control how we respond to the choices of others we don't agree with, and we can make the choices in our own lives that align with the truths that matter to us. We can stop interacting with messages of hate, and we can start seeing opportunities for healing no matter where our gaze might fall. We can wait and feel annoyed about how long it's taking, or we can use that time of waiting to reflect on whatever beauty can be found in the people or creatures or natural spaces with whom we are sharing space.

So even while the climate changes and we wait for things to get back to normal in a world that has stretched normal to its limits, and while we hope for change that may or may not come into being in our lifetime, we don't have to be stagnant. We can be active in our waiting. We can practice peace, we can be the light, and we can see the beauty and good tidings even while mosquitoes hatch in December and Santa has to travel by boat.

Color Vision

The snow is sparkling as I glide forward across the deserted lake, finally frozen now in the depths of winter. Bright sun glints off each individual snowflake, and the reeds shift in a gentle breeze. There are tracks of small creatures who came this way before I did, and I wonder if we'll ever cross paths, even once removed, again. It is eerily still. Quiet. The thermometer says it's -10, and if the news media is to be believed, you'd be foolish to even think about venturing outside into such frigid, inhospitable air.

To be fair, those who are without warm shelter or adequate winter wear undoubtedly suffer on days like this. To be homeless or in need of heat in the winter in Minnesota is something no one should have to experience. I am thankful for a warm house, a wood stove and poly fiber clothing—skiing across a frozen lake in negative temperatures would be a very different experience without them.

But since I do have those things, they color my perception of beauty on this day. There is beauty in the way the air pierces your breath and leaves it hanging just a moment longer in the stillness. There is beauty in the solitude that can be found when you leave the house and meld into a version of nature where your only companions are the birds who never seem to mind the cold. There is beauty in the blueness of the sky above the landscape of blinding white.

Sometimes I wonder if anyone else can see how blue the sky is on days like this. Maybe it's just vivid blue when so many forget to look, or when so many can't see because they are just trying to survive.

From inside the warm house, the snow is still sparkling, and the sun is still shining brightly down on the still and frozen waters of this land. The sky is still blue, but through the window it is less vivid. I wonder if I imagined its vibrancy before, or if in coming back into the house—away from the version of nature that includes birds and the creatures who left tracks before I did—I left part of my color vision outside the door.

Perhaps it's not so foolish to venture out if it means you can see more clearly, if even just for a moment.

Teachers in the Rocks

Yesterday I took to the woods in the afternoon. It's the first time in about ten years when I don't have any sort of schedule. There is no work calendar hovering in the background, I'm not on vacation for a certain amount of time, there are no appointments to plan around. I'm a free agent, at least for now. So I did what I do when I can do whatever I want—I went to the woods.

Going to the woods is what I tend to do when I am feeling melancholy, unsure, anxious, or angry. It's a place to go when I'm grieving, wondering, lamenting, or stewing about something outside of my control. Basically, going to the woods (or prairie, or ocean, or any other natural area) is healing. It's a place to go in celebration as well, but lately, its role in my days has been one of holding space for what needs to rise from the ashes of what has recently burnt away.

There's a waterfall on the edge of one of the state parks close to my house. It's fed by a natural spring, and the grounds where it sits used to be the old Silverbrook estate and laboratory, now only evident in some old stone foundations and crumbling pillars. I hiked down the steep trail from the access road to the spring as a gentle dusting of snow fell, the cold wind piercing my skin and whistling through the white pine trees that dot the landscape. I watched the crystal clear water bubble up from the earth for a while, meandered around the pond full of bright green watercress, and felt myself melt into the rhythm of the forest as I walked deeper into the trees. After emerging from the forest trail, I made my way over to the waterfall and marveled at its powerful cascades as they crashed into the rocky ravine below. I followed the waterfall's creek further down the ravine to the St. Croix River and watched it fade into the larger body of water, now partially frozen as the cold temperatures take hold. As I hiked back up to the main trail, I looked to my right and stopped.

There on the larger boulders on either side of the creek, someone had built three huge rock cairns. The largest was closest to the trail, and it was taller than me, the stones increasingly smaller as they found balance on their neighbor. And the stone on top was huge, yet there it was, perched just so and not going anywhere. The other two were closer to the stream of cascading water, and smaller but no less well-balanced, the stones in varying sizes and shapes, each placed in exactly the right spot to maintain the structure. I could imagine the person who made the cairns searching for just the right rocks to place, and then one by one patiently placing each stone in just the right way. I imagined that it probably took quite awhile to construct each one, and I found myself wondering how long they'd last. I wondered how many times they toppled before the right balance was found.

Somehow seeing these rock cairns reminded me of the things that can help with regaining balance in a time of searching through murky waters or walking over a path strewn with erratic boulders. They reminded me of the patience it can take to create something that works. They reminded me of the delicate and often unusual beauty that pervades everything in nature and in a human life. They reminded me that things can shift instantly, in any direction. They reminded me that there is a lot that remains outside of my control and that I often don't get a say in what happens. And they reminded me that I get to choose what sorts of things I want in my life, whether it's in the form of perception or situation, and they reminded me I get to place my own rocks where they need to be to feel solid. Even if they fall sometimes, and even when what used to feel like the "right balance" shifts.

I came to the woods to lose myself in the rhythm of the woods and waterfall, and I did. But I also gained some reassurance that the right balance doesn't always look how I think it should, and it can take a while to find the placement of the pieces that make up a life.

The Art of Living Wild

We set out from the retreat house as the temperature hovered around one below zero. The winter sunshine filtered through the cracks of the skeleton trees, and we walked across a quiet barnyard, past a red barn and trickled into single file as our steps faded into the snowy trail into the woods. The occasional cry of a hawk, the squeak of the cold snow underfoot and the muted whisperings of the winter forest were the only sounds piercing the air. Our breath left our bodies in clouds of white vapor with every exhale, and we drank in the deep clean cold like a tonic. We skirted the edge of a deep ravine, climbed over old tired logs and stopped to listen to the spring fed creek, still full of life and green watercress on this frozen day in January. We took the path up onto the edge of the site of ancient burial grounds, gazed across the frozen oak savanna and headed back down into the ravine toward the rushing water. The waterfall, even in the frigid grasp of winter, called out in welcome as its water cascaded in icy blasts that we could hear as we approached. We pushed our boundaries with a precarious crossing, picking our way one at a time over a thin rock bridge that boasts step drop offs on either side and gasped in amazement as we looked up from our foot placement and into a wall of blue and green ice that forms each year as the groundwater seeps and flows downward, freezing as it goes. The waterfall crashed, the creek water ran, the sun sparkled brightly on the ice formations, and we marveled in the beauty and power of the wild tapestry before us. We thought briefly about wading in the crystal clear water, and then we thought better of it and continued on our hike, fueled by a new kind of energy that comes straight from the core of the earth.

In addition to the frosty hike, the rest of the weekend long retreat was spent in yoga, in breathwork, in meditation, in visioning, in free form dance, in enjoying nourishing food, and in fellowship. It was a weekend of celebrating the wild nature that is deeply rooted in every woman and of giving voice to the desires that call from the soul. It was a weekend of telling the story that needs to be told to move into the life that is ours to live. It was a weekend of claiming the right to choose the things that call instead of the things that beckon; to claim the clarity that listening to the deep and quiet and fiery and passionate parts of ourselves can offer. It was a weekend to put aside the stories of anxiety, of fear, of constriction; to put aside the stories of want and pick up the stories of need. It was a weekend to acknowledge the beauty and strength that we all have and don't always let ourselves see. It was a weekend to leave the cage behind to remember how to howl and sing just because we can. Because the world needs our authentic, wild voices now more than ever.

Clarissa Pinkola Estes writes, "The way to maintain one's connection to the wild is to ask yourself what it is that you want. This is the sorting of the seed from the dirt. One of the most important discriminations we can make in this matter is the difference between things that beckon to us and things that call from our souls."

Dr. Estes goes on to say, "Nature does not ask permission." She's right, of course. Nature just is, authentically and without apologies. That waterfall that we hiked to didn't ask anybody if it was allowed to thunder down the side of a hill and carve a deep ravine into the landscape. This weekend retreat was an opportunity to take a cue from mother nature herself and stop asking for permission to be. It was a time to remember that what is enough for us will always be changing but the fact that we are enough will always be truth.

Living wildly is an art and one of the most beautiful pieces of work one can ever undertake.

Jars of Bliss

On the surface, there's not much going on with gardens in Minnesota right now. It's January, the temperature outside has been consistently below zero, and the view up the hill to the field is awash with brown, gray and bright white. The hoses are wound and covered with piles of snow, the berry bushes have turned brittle with the cold and the garlic that was planted a few months ago lays in wait for the spring thaw that is still months away. A few seed catalogues have arrived, some pots have been moved to a different spot in the garage, and we continue to add to the compost pile at the delight of the opossum that lives nearby, but activities like baking bread, starting fires in the wood stove, skiing around the lake and reading books dictate the flow of the days. There is the coming season's garden to plan, to be sure.... but it feels early, yet.

But despite the lack of growth outside right now, we do still have to eat. This afternoon in search of a snack, I reached up into the pantry past the graham crackers, granola and oatmeal to where all of the produce that we put up last fall is stored. I pulled out a tiny jar full of slender green beans—they were packed in tight, nestled in between garlic cloves and sprigs of dill.

Popping the top off and fishing out the first bean brought me instantly to the screen porch of my parents' house where we spent a long weekend last September harvesting, washing, chopping, mixing, cooking, stirring and packing into jars and freezer bags all sorts of home-grown abundance. These canning weekends are always a lot of work, the days are long, there are dogs and toddlers running around underfoot, and every counter or tabletop is a disaster area of discarded food scraps, spills, dirty dishes and heaps of unprocessed produce. Food preservation is not an elegant business when you do it in bulk with a family of farmers. But at the end of these weekends, our bellies full of home cooking and laughter, we load up the car with boxes and bags full of canned tomatoes, beans, jam, salsa and beets plus a cooler full of all the things we froze, or plan to later, like pesto and kale and corn to enjoy in the cold dark months of winter that are yet to come. Preservation days are long and a lot of work—but despite the labor, we mourn the swiftly passing time while we celebrate and give thanks for the goodness that we have.

I ate the dilly beans this afternoon for a snack, savoring the freshness and light that was preserved all those months ago. There's not much happening on the surface out in the gardens right now, but the energy of taking care of the land by living close to the earth and existing in a way that uses what we have to meet our needs shines through every jar or freezer bag that provides a foundation for a winter meal.

The New World of Winter

This winter started early with a foot of unexpected snow in mid-November, and then 13 days later temperatures in the 40s and 50s invited the ground to turn dry and brown again. Then a few weeks into December, the temperature dropped below freezing, and it snowed just enough inches to cover the ground in bright white. We got a few weeks of ice skating on the rink that my husband likes to clear on the lake, skied some loops around the field in shallow tracks, and our almost three year old took her first runs down the sledding hill through the wisps of grass that poked through the snow cover. Then it got bitterly cold, and we woke up to wind chills of twenty below zero for a week straight. And now, at the end of January, the temperature is 40 degrees, the sun is out and the snow is succumbing to the heat once again. We made a snowman, and he's shrinking as I type this. I'm not sure he'll make it a full week. My skis are languishing by the back door, despondent in their respite from use. The snowshoes are sitting by the door, waiting to be needed.

The last few years I've noticed that winter is no longer the winter I knew in my childhood. Winters of my youth on the South Dakota prairie were cold, snow-filled and windy. Snow days were a given every year, and I got stuck driving home on early release days in my rear wheel drive car more than once in high school. Massive snow forts ruled the yard and fields across the road, and my brothers and I did our best not to break a leg trying to use cross-country skis to slalom down the hill behind the house. Ice skating on the frozen river runoff channels to "Lost Lake" (aka a cattle pond) defined the afternoons and weekends for months on end. Frozen toes, icy eyelashes and red cheeks were the norm. Snow and below freezing temperatures came in December and stayed until March. There were surely warmer years and colder years, and some unusual weather during those times, but it feels different now. Now the ice forms and thaws, I've started to expect rain in December, and snow falls and melts away before we can get our bearings. There are no massive snow forts in my current rural Minnesota neighborhood. This freeze and melt cycle keeps repeating, creating conditions that are unpredictable and different than I want them to be.

Sandra Steingraber writes, "Meanwhile, a friend calls to tell me that her otherwise very bright granddaughter, who is of nursery-school age, is having trouble learning the names of the seasons. They make no sense to her. 'But grandma, you said that winter was cold!' Winter, when she said it, wasn't. And there was the added problem of the forsythias. They bloomed this year during a warm spell that spanned the twelve days of Christmas. April showers bring May flowers. When the nursery rhymes no longer match the empirical evidence, what's a three-year-old to think?"

It's no secret that the climate is different now than it was in the 1980s when I was a child. It continues to change as I type these words, and our human culture as a whole doesn't know how to make the choices and changes to do what is necessary to start to heal what's broken. There are those who say it's beyond healing and we are headed for crisis, no matter what we do. There are those who say that if everyone would just change their light bulbs, we'd be moving the right direction. There are those who say "why bother?" when they realize the minimal impact changing a light bulb has in the face of what truly needs to happen to right the course the earth is on. There are those who disengage from culture and try to live off the ever powerful grid in every possible way. There are those who holler and fast and chain themselves to bulldozers to try to win a battle in a war that seems like it will never end.

Yet even those of us who know the facts and find them compelling and important still write blog posts on computers made with non-biodegradable plastic parts that are powered by the fossil fuel that needs to stay in the ground for things to have any hope of taking a positive turn. Even those who are committed fully to living in a way that is life-giving and sustainable for ALL life on the planet still find themselves traveling by automobile or drinking water that has been piped in across a desert or unexpectedly navigating a situation where the only option is to choose the lesser of two evils.

So. I've noticed that winters look and feel different than they did 25 years ago and that it's probably not going to back to how it was then. A lot of people have noticed that, I think. I don't know the answers on how to change the trajectory of the culture in which we live. But I do know that we have the answers somewhere, even if I won't see them play out in my lifetime. That's what keeps me changing my light bulbs and saving money for solar panels and planting an organic garden: The hope that the answers that are buried within the human collective—within the planet itself—will start to make their way into the freeze and thaw cycles that are so disorienting and feel so raw.

When we start to look for the answers in the discomfort of the unknown, we will be better equipped to see what way to go from here.

Illustration

Like Cassandra howling at the gates of Troy, bear witness to what you know to be true. Tell the truths that have been bent by skilled advertising. Tell the truths that have been concealed by adroit regulations. Tell the truths that have been denied by fear or complacency. Go to the tar fields, go to the broken pipelines. Tell that story. Be the noisy gong and clanging cymbals, and be the love.

–KATHLEEN DEAN MOORE

As another winter holds my part of the earth in a cold embrace, I have found myself waiting for things—the big things of life, like laws and politics and the notion that war is inevitable—to be different. I have been hopeful for a new way of being in the world. I have been waiting for something to shift, for something to be reset, for something to tell me that "Yes, now it is time." To tell me, "Be who you really are. It's ok to truly stand up for what matters." I have been waiting and hoping for validation, for something bigger than my own mind to let me know that I can do things differently. I have been waiting for my culture to wake up and see the world beyond what is presented via propaganda. I have been waiting for things to be different.

And now I am still waiting, in a sense. I am no longer placing my hopes on something that may or may not happen, but I wait none the less. It is not clear what I am waiting for anymore. Perhaps I'm waiting for someone to say it's alright to take action, or for an event to take place that will make action essential, or for an option to appear that feels realistic—or one that allows me to stay comfortable. Maybe I am waiting for the sign that says "go" instead of deciding for myself when the time is right to begin. Perhaps things are different but I haven't allowed them to take a deep breath and exhale into being.

And then again, if I look deeper, I can see that every moment has been essential in my journey, even if I don't know exactly where I am headed. Being elsewhere right now isn't where I am supposed to be. There is validation in accepting the present and in seeing the beauty that lives in the imperfection of my current life situation. A new way of being in the world is alive when I remember that I already see with clear eyes and when I acknowledge the power in that.

Yet the quandary remains: There is still so much beauty that is being destroyed in the world, so much pain, so much aching. There is so much longing for something different and so much hope that something will shift. I've been waiting for things to be different, and right now I am sensing the urgency of this waiting. There ceases to be time reserved for waiting just in case something happens. There is a place for hopeful expectation, yes. But to use Professor Murphy's words again, "Hope is not wishful thinking; it is risk and action and the courage to undertake both."

Right now there is only the call to tell the truth—and to take the risk to do what I sense the world is asking. As Gandhi once said, to be repeated by millions, "I need to be the change I want to see in the world."

Afterword

Listen
To everything there is a season,
a time for every purpose under the sun.
—Ecclesiastes 3:1

I look out the back door into the sunrise.

I listen.

There is a faint, yet unwavering beat spreading horizontally over the landscape. It has a rhythm like the powwows of the Lakota people, of a drumming circle, of a collective chanting and funneling of energy into a medium that can be felt and heard by all. This pulse is coming from Gaia, from the core of the earth, from the Being that is represented in all life on the planet. It cannot be ignored. It can be pushed aside and is by many, but it is persistent. The authentic earth is speaking.

What do we hear? What are we going to do with this pulse that is reminding us of who we are? What are we going to be as the ancient rhythm settles into our veins and spreads outward through our choices?

Through our choices, by the actions we take and because of the way we walk on the earth, we are part of the life that continues to unfold all around us. Nothing that is life—that has the capacity to love, that is the essence of something bigger than we can fully understand—can be contained by systems that are not peace centered and life giving. Though we have plenty of broken systems, we as a collective are an integral part of the unwavering beat—the pulse—and the energy that is propelling our world into something that we know is truth. To something that is more beautiful than we can imagine on the good days.

This forward motion, this horizontal push into the newness of what has always been at the core, is not without challenge. Change is hard for humans, even when the change is full of light and promise. It can be easy to hold on to what we know, even when it doesn't serve who we truly are. Even while we welcome change, we don't know what our reality will look like in the days to come, and we have a hard time with the unknowing. We want something concrete; we want dates to look forward to. We want to plan, and we want to see changes and energy shifts manifest in ways that we can understand and see in our daily lives.

We will get these things, even when it feels like we are still waiting for a sign that now we can truly live how we are meant to live. Because while we question, while we still feel like we are waiting, while we strive to exist in a way that is authentic, the pulse is still there. It has always been there. Many ears are still deaf to the realness of the beating, but it is getting louder with every intention to live as a part of the whole and to be as one with the heart of creation.

I look out the back door into the sunrise. I feel the pulse of the earth and the turning of the season. I hear the collective call to be a people of wholeness and of healing.

Listen.

Be part of the sunrise.

Acknowledgements

Where to begin when giving thanks? There is always more to say that we humans know how to convey in words. As the saying goes, it takes a village—to raise a child, but also to do many other things in life, like publish a book. First and foremost, thank you to Julia LeNeau—you said the words, "let's start a blog" back in 2008, and I don't know if I would have started writing again had you not gotten the ball rolling. I will always think of our camping adventure to Interstate park as the event that invited me to reclaim writing. Thank you to Ellie, Amelia, Susan, Mary Beth, Kris, and the other contributors to the Enough blog—this little core of female writers has fed me in so many ways and led to some of the content of this book. Thank you to Gail—your encouragement to submit a query was instrumental in getting this collection of essays from word document to book, and I am forever grateful for your support and the fact that you were willing to read the manuscript of someone you didn't really even know at the time. (Thanks Bill for the introduction!) Thanks to Kevin and Alissa of *We Are Wildness*—you continue to inspire me to live close to the earth, and I will always value the opportunities that have come from our connection. Thank you to my little community of neighbors and friends in America's Little Sweden and the surrounding river valley—community is an essential part of being on earth, so thank you for being mine. Thank you to Leslie Browning and Homebound Publications, for believing in this project and providing the opportunity to get it out into the world.

Thank you to my family: To my parents for taking me to the woods as a young child and teaching me that being outside is as essential as breathing for a full life; to my brothers and their partners for being willing participants in adventures of all sorts over the years. And above all, thank you to Nick and Eva. Wherever our choices take us next, I'm forever grateful for your love and support. Without your presence in my life, these words would never have come into being.

Bibliography

Benz, Inelia; Fear Processing Exercise, www.acension101.com.

Berry, Wendell. *Jayber Crow: The Life Story of Jayber Crow, Barber, of the Port William*

Membership, as Written by Himself. *Thorndike, Me.:* Thorndike, 2001. Print.

Burkeman, Oliver. *The Antidote: Happiness for People Who Can't Stand Positive Thinking.* New York: Faber and Faber, 2012. Print.

Demeter, Staff. "Biodynamic Principles and Practices." Http:// www.demeter-usa.org/learn-more/biodynamic-principles-practices.asp. Demeter USA, 2016. Web.

Essmaker, Tina. "Krista Tippett on *The Great Discontent* (TGD)." The Great Discontent. 16 Sept. 2016. Web.

Estes, Clarissa Pinkola. *Women Who Run with the Wolves: Myths and Stories of the Wild Woman Archetype.* New York: Ballantine, 1992. Print.

Francis, "Laudato Si' (24 May 2015)." Laudato Si' (24 May 2015) | Francis. Web.

Jensen, Derrick. "Against Forgetting." *Orion Magazine* Aug. 2013. Print.

Lamott, Anne. *Stitches: A Handbook on Meaning, Hope and Repair.* New York: Riverhead , a Member of Penguin Group (USA), 2013. Print.

Mark 13:36. Adapted. *The New Oxford Annotated Bible.* New York: Oxford UP, 2001. Print.

Moore, Kathleen Dean. *Wild Comfort: The Solace of Nature.* Boston, MA: Trumpeter, 2010. Print.

Murphy, D. D. *Would That You Might Meet Us Doing Right.* On Being. 30 November, 2014. Web.

North House Folk School: a non-profit that focuses on teaching traditional northern crafts, building community, and fostering creativity and inter-generational learning, www.northhouse.org.

O'Rourke, Meghan. *The Long Goodbye*. New York: Riverhead, 2011. Print.

Oliver, Mary. *Upstream*. Penguin Press, 2016. Pg 5.

Oschman, James, @mercola Mercola. "Dr. James Oschman: Earthing Can Do Wonders to Your Health." Mercola.com. 29 Apr. 2012. Web.

Quinn, Daniel. *Ishmael*. New York: Bantam/Turner Book, 1995. Print.

Safi, Omid. "Where Does It Hurt, O City of Light." On Being. 15 Nov. 2015.

Simondes, Hema. "Come to Your Senses through Grounding." Earthrunners.com. Earth Runners, 24 Nov. 2014. Web.

Stafford, William. *The Way it Is: New and Selected Poems*. Graywolf Press, 1998.

Steingraber, Sandra. "The Discontent of Our Winter." *Orion Magazine*, April 2013. Print.

Storyhill. "Blazing Out of Sight." Lyrics. Storyhill Red House Records, 2007.

HOMEBOUND PUBLICATIONS

Ensuring that the mainstream isn't the only stream.

At Homebound Publications, we publish books written by independent voices for independent minds. Our books focus on a return to simplicity and balance, connection to the earth and each other, and the search for meaning and authenticity.

Founded in 2011, Homebound Publications is one of the rising independent publishers in the country. Collectively through our imprints, we publish between fifteen to twenty offerings each year. Our authors have received dozens of awards including: *Foreword Reviews'* Book of the Year, Nautilus Book Award, Benjamin Franklin Book Awards, and Saltire Literary Awards. Highly-respected among bookstores, readers and authors alike, Homebound Publications has a proven devotion to quality, originality and integrity.

We are a small press with big ideas. As an independent publisher we strive to ensure that the mainstream is not the only stream. It is our intention at Homebound Publications to preserve contemplative storytelling. We publish full-length introspective works of creative nonfiction, essay collections, travel writing, and novels. In all our titles, our intention is to introduce new perspectives that will directly aid humankind in the trials we face at present as a global village.

WWW.HOMEBOUNDPUBLICATIONS.COM